with

I0002982

DANGERS ON THE INTERNET

STAYING SAFE ON-LINE

Kevin F. Rothman

The Rosen Publishing Group, Inc.
New York

Published in 2001 by The Rosen Publishing Group, Inc.
29 East 21st Street, New York, NY 10010

Copyright © 2001 by Kevin F. Rothman

First Edition

All rights reserved. No part of this book may be reproduced in any form without permission in writing from the publisher, except by a reviewer.

Cover photo © Archive Photography

Library of Congress Cataloging-in-Publication Data

Rothman, Kevin F.
    Coping with dangers on the Internet: staying safe on-line / by Kevin F. Rothman.
        p.   cm.
    Includes bibliographical references and index.
    Contents: An introduction to the Internet—General safety guidelines—Sending and receiving email—Surfing the world wide Web—Chatrooms, newsgroups, and mailing lists—Publishing on the Web.
        ISBN: 978-1-4358-8650-6

    1. Internet and teenages 2. Internet—Safety measures 3. World Wide Web. I. Title.
    HQ799.2.I5R67   2000
    025.04'0835—dc21   00-010322

Manufactured in the United States of America

About the Author

Kevin F. Rothman earned a B.A. from Yale University, has worked as a professional Web developer, and currently attends law school in New York City. He was born in Michigan and has lived in Switzerland, Singapore, Germany, and the United States.

To my family, and to Maia

Contents

1 An Introduction to the Internet   1

2 General Safety Guidelines   10

3 Sending and Receiving E-Mail   39

4 Surfing the World Wide Web   70

5 Chat Rooms, Newsgroups, and Mailing Lists   93

6 Publishing on the Web   106

Glossary   113

Where to Go for Help   115

For Further Reading   118

Index   119

An Introduction to
the Internet

You have probably already used the Internet—for school research, for downloading music or computer games, or for sending and receiving e-mail—or know someone who has. Whatever your experience with the Internet is, you should realize that along with the many wonderful things it does for us, it can also be a source of danger.

The Internet

Think of the Internet as a big city. A big city contains great places to visit—museums, historical sites, and shopping centers—as well as bad parts of town. The best way to protect yourself from wandering into these dangerous "parts" of the Internet is to understand what the Internet is and how it works.

When some people think of the Internet, commonly known as the Net, they think of Web pages. Others think of e-mail. Still others think of chat rooms. If you don't know what these things are, don't worry. They are all explained in this book. If you do know what these things are, it's important to realize that they are merely parts of the Internet. The Internet is a global structure that moves different kinds of information from one place to another, usually between computers. Let's take a closer look.

The Infrastructure

Information, or data, travels over the Internet much like water travels through a plumbing system. There are high-speed lines, collectively called the Internet backbone, that carry the bulk of the data. These lines are like the large pipes that form the basis of a plumbing system. Internet hubs, devices used as connection points, link up the high-speed lines. At the time of the writing of this book, 85 percent of Internet data in the United States is carried through the backbone lines running from the Internet hub in Virginia, MAE-EAST, to the Internet hub in California, MAE-WEST.

In the United States, the Internet backbone is made up mainly of fiber-optic cables running through the ground. Fiber-optic cabling also runs under the oceans to connect the United States to Europe, South Africa, and parts of Asia and South America. Internet data, however, may also travel through other systems. For instance, most of "wired" Africa is connected via a satellite backbone. A portion of the data traveling between the United States and Europe is also carried by satellites.

Springing off of the backbone (and the hubs) are various smaller networks. In the United States, these networks connect various towns and cities to the Internet. Many companies, schools, and organizations are directly connected to the Internet as well.

People tend to connect to the Internet through ISPs, or internet service providers. One well-known example of an Internet Service Provider is America Online, or AOL. (AOL also functions as more than an ISP.) People who want to use the Internet will connect to their ISP, and the ISP will connect them to the Internet.

There are several ways to connect to an ISP. A popular way is to use a computer modem to dial up to the ISP over a telephone line. If you have used this kind of connection before, you will notice that you have to wait to connect to the Internet, and you may hear strange noises while you wait. This connection may also seem slow. The fastest connection speed using this method at the time of the writing of this book is 56 kilobits per second.

It is also possible to connect to an ISP through a cable television system, or through a service called DSL, or digital subscriber line. These methods typically offer faster connection speeds than a traditional modem—up to 100 times faster—and often do not require a user to sign on or wait to connect to the Internet. Yet another way to connect to the Internet is through a cellular phone, which is sometimes called a cell phone, or through any other device that uses the same method as a cellular phone, such as a PDA, or personal digital assistant. A popular PDA is the Palm Pilot.

Devices that Connect to the Internet

There are many devices that connect to the Internet, and every day someone is working on a new one. Some of the more popular devices are described below.

Personal Computers

Most people connect to the Internet using a personal computer, or PC. PCs are what most people think of when they hear the word "computer." A typical desktop PC has several parts to it. There is the monitor, or computer screen, which is like a television screen. There is also the CPU box, which is the box that holds the central processing unit (such as an Intel Pentium processor), as well as various drives, such as the hard drive, floppy disk drive, and CD-ROM drive. Additionally, there are input devices, such as a keyboard and mouse. Most desktop PCs also have a modem for connecting to the Internet.

Personal Digital Assistants

Personal digital assistants, or PDAs, are small, handheld devices that people use for storing addresses, keeping schedules, and other functions. Many PDAs are also able to access the Internet through a wireless connection. Because of their small screen size, PDAs lend themselves best to e-mail and simple Web sites.

Netappliances

Appliances created solely for e-mail and Web surfing are called netappliances. These appliances differ from PCs because they are not capable of performing significant non–on-line tasks, such as word processing. They are called netappliances because they are similar to traditional appliances such as toaster ovens in the sense that they are inexpensive and dedicated to only a handful of tasks.

One example of a netappliance is the WebTV set-top box, which connects to a television set to allow the user to perform e-mail and Web surfing tasks. At first glance, this device appears similar to a PC—there is a screen, keyboard, and mouse. This device, however, differs significantly from a PC in that there is no hard drive and the device cannot run computer programs such as a word processor or spreadsheet program. Some netappliances also double as video game consoles and personal television recorders.

Mobile Phones

Mobile phones, commonly called cell phones, allow people to have a telephone connection from pretty much anywhere. Many cellular phones also allow access to the Internet. For example, they can be used to check e-mail.

Future Devices

People have begun to connect to the Internet using devices installed in their cars. Because it is dangerous to drive and look at a computer screen at the same time, these devices use computer voices that read e-mail and Web site text aloud. Some people envision a world where almost every electronic device, like a watch, for example, is somehow connected to the Internet.

Protocols

The Internet began in the 1960s as ARPANET. (ARPANET took its name from the Defense Department's Advanced Research Project Agency NETwork.) The ARPANET was built as an alternative communications medium in the event of a nuclear war. The United States was worried that if attacked with nuclear missiles by the former Soviet Union, its telephone system would be rendered useless.

TCP/IP

One of the first ways that scientists came up with to move information across the Internet was TCP/IP. (TCP/IP stands for transmission control protocol/internet protocol.) A protocol is a set of rules for how two computers speak to one another through a modem or network. TCP/IP is an example of a process called packet switching. Packet switching involves breaking up into small chunks the information to be moved across a network.

Say, for example, that you wanted to send the following message to someone on the Internet: "howdy." A program operating according to a packet switching protocol might divide up the message into individual letters: h, o, w, d, and y. Each individual letter would be called a packet. The program would then send each packet, or letter, to the message recipient. Once the packets arrived, a program on the recipient's end would take the packets and reassemble them into the original message ("howdy"). TCP controls how the packets are created and IP controls how the packets get to their destination.

E-Mail
Once TCP/IP was in place, a number of new ways to send information over the Internet utilizing TCP/IP were developed. One of the most common ways to send information—one that you may have tried before—is through something called electronic mail, or e-mail. E-mail can work in many different ways—messages can be sent within a company network or between pagers or cellular phones. The most common way, however, is for someone to type a message along with an e-mail address into a computer, and then to send that message over the Internet. The message then waits to be picked up by the person who has the e-mail address to which the message was sent.

World Wide Web

The World Wide Web (WWW) is a collection of linked documents that use the hypertext transfer protocol (HTTP) and the hypertext markup language (HTML). Some of the phrases associated with the WWW are the Web, Web pages, Web sites, sites, home pages, links, bookmarks, favorites, browsers, Netscape, Internet Explorer, and hypertext. Any time you access an address like http://www.disney.com, you are retrieving a document on the WWW, or the Web.

Web Sites

The Web uses a metaphor of linked pages called Web pages, which are accessed using a tool called a browser. Microsoft Internet Explorer and Netscape Communicator are examples of browsers. Web pages are collected into groups called Web sites. Oftentimes a Web site may be associated with a particular domain name, such as mtv.com. Other examples of domain names are microsoft.com, whitehouse.gov, and pbs.org. When you access a Web site, you usually put "www" before the domain name.

A particular place on the Internet, such as a particular Web page, and the associated protocol can be described with something called a universal resource locator (URL). An example of a URL is http://www.fbi.gov/mostwanted, the FBI's "America's Most Wanted" Web page. This URL specifies both a location (www.fbi.gov/mostwanted) and a protocol (http, or hypertext transfer protocol).

Applications

The Web began with Web pages that simply displayed infor-mation. These were called static Web pages. After some time, the Web pages became interactive—they would accept input from a user and output a response. For example, if you input a search term into a search engine, the search engine will output (send back to you) links to Web pages containing the search term. Today, people are work-ing to develop Web-based applications, which are accessed with a browser and take the place of traditional computer programs. For example, you can use your browser to check e-mail, to play games, or to chat on a Web site. In the past, these tasks required separate programs. In the future, people expect that many applications, such as word processors and graphics programs, will be accessed using a browser.

Other Internet Areas

Other areas of the Internet that you should know about (and that are discussed in greater detail later in this book) are chat rooms, instant messaging, newsgroups, mailing lists, and file-sharing programs.

Chat Rooms

Chat rooms are areas on the Internet where people can communicate instantly by typing on their computers and where everyone in the "room" can see what everyone else is typing.

Instant Messaging

Instant messaging is a way for two people to create a pri-vate chat room using two computers. If you receive an instant message from someone, the message typically pops up on your computer screen.

Newsgroups

Newsgroups, sometimes called bulletin boards or forums, are on-line discussion groups. Comments are "posted" by users to the newsgroup. Once a comment has been posted, it remains on the newsgroup so other users can visit the newsgroup at their leisure to read the comment and post replies.

Mailing Lists

A mailing list is a collection of individual e-mail addresses identified by a single mailing list address. When an e-mail is sent to the mailing list address, it is automatically forwarded to all of the individual addresses. To add his or her individual address to a mailing list, a person has to "subscribe" to the list.

File-sharing Programs

File-sharing programs allow people connected to the Internet to directly share files on their hard drives. A popular file-sharing program is Gnutella, which allows users to share mp3 files on their hard drives. File-sharing programs, however, can be used to share any type of file, not just mp3 files.

General Safety Guidelines

The technology that runs the Internet today was designed with an open network in mind, meaning that anyone could access it. On one hand, this openness is wonderful because it allows everyone to exchange information easily and thus to become true "netizens," citizens of the Internet. On the other hand, however, this openness can create serious security threats.

As you use the Internet, you will come across many situations where you could make you or your family vulnerable by not taking proper security measures. For example, you may choose a password that is easy to guess, download a program that contains a virus, or give out credit card information.

New technologies are introduced on the Internet every day. If you come across situations where you suspect—even in a very minor way—that your security or privacy may be at risk, tell your parents, and ask them to contact a technical person at your ISP for help.

Choosing Passwords

Passwords are the most common security tool used in cyberspace. Sites should always give you an opportunity to choose your password. Even if you are preassigned a password, nearly all programs that would require you to log in will provide a way for you to change this password.

You should choose a password that is easy for you to remember but is difficult for others to guess. Also, you should include both numbers and letters in your password. Avoid choosing a password that is generic, like "password," or a password that is easy to guess, like your birthday.

To understand why, let's look at how an amateur hacker typically attempts to break into someone's password-protected account. A hacker—or more properly, a "cracker"—is someone who tries to gain unauthorized access to computer systems.

All week, Christina had been trying to come up with a way to get back at Paul. She was mad at him because he hadn't asked her to the homecoming dance, even though he told Masha, her best friend, that he had planned to. Instead, he had asked Deb, a new girl at school.

Christina was usually a pretty honest person, but this time her emotions got the better of her. She decided to break into Paul's e-mail account and fake an embarrassing e-mail from Paul to Deb. Christina knew that Paul's e-mail address was different_sundays@isp.com, so she guessed that his username might be different_sundays. (She was right.)

In order to log in as Paul, Christina needed to know his password. First she tried a bunch of obvious ones. They are listed on the next page. Can you see why the passwords listed are obvious?

password	springfield (Paul's birthplace)
password1	bmw (Paul's favorite car)
sparky (Paul's dog)	paul
sparky1	paul1
oasis (Paul's favorite band)	tina (Paul's ex-girlfriend)
oasis1	secret
different_sundays	secret1
different_sundays1	12345
010782 (Paul's birthday)	
january7	

None of these passwords worked. Next, Christina downloaded a program called a "brute force password cracker." This program would try every word from any dictionary Christina gave it. She loaded Webster's Standard English Dictionary into the program and let it run overnight. By morning, the program had tried over a million passwords, but none of them had worked.

Christina knew Paul liked comic books, so she downloaded a comic book dictionary and loaded it into the program. Within ten minutes, the program discovered Paul's password. The password was "Aquaman," one of Paul's favorite comics. Christina then began to write a fake e-mail from Paul to Deb. "Dear Deb," it began. "I'm excited to go to homecoming with you. I just wanted to let you know in advance that I don't use deodorant. Most people don't mind, but I just didn't want to shock you." After Christina wrote the e-mail, however, she realized that what she did not only sounded stupid but was also very wrong.

Christina told her parents and Paul everything that she had done. Because she had been honest, her parents let her off easy (she was grounded for two weekends) and she avoided serious trouble. But she certainly didn't impress Paul much. He told her that it would be a long time before he could trust her again.

As you can see from this scenario, people who hack e-mail programs have both simple and sophisticated methods of figuring out someone's password. Being aware of hacker methods will help you choose a password wisely.

Tricks to Choosing a Password

One great way to choose a password is to use the first letter of every word of a phrase you can remember, and then add a number. For example, let's say that a phrase you can easily remember is "To be or not to be," and a number you can remember is 17. Your password would be "tbontb17." Do you see how this works? "To be or not to be" + 17.

Another way to obtain a secure password is to use a random string generator. These generators create random "strings" of letters and numbers, such as "ksj3hdi8." Random strings are extremely difficult to guess, but they are also usually quite difficult for users to remember.

Random string generator programs that run on your computer can be easily downloaded from the Internet. If you do not want to download a program, you can visit one of the many Web pages that will create a random string for you.

Have More than One Password

However you choose your password, if you decide to write it down, put it in a safe place that is not near your computer or in a place where someone would think to look. Also, do not use the same password for everything. You should have at least three passwords: a "general" one you use often for programs and Web sites that are insignificant (such as a free games Web site), a "medium security" one you use sparingly for more important programs and Web sites (such as an e-mail Web site like hotmail.com), and a "high security" one you use only for your most important programs and Web sites (such as an on-line banking Web site).

There are computer programs that keep a list of all of your existing passwords and require one master password to access the list. Some of these programs are on the World Wide Web, whereas others are applications that you keep on your computer. Using one of these programs that exists on the Web is not a good idea because if someone guesses your master password, he or she will have access to the list of all of your passwords!

Using one of these programs that is stored on your computer can be quite secure, but before you use such a program, make sure that only you or people you trust will have access to your computer.

Change Your Password Often

The longer you use the same password, the more opportunities you create for someone else to steal it. For this reason, you should change your password on a regular basis. Passwords for critical applications, such as your e-mail or bank account, should be changed often—at least once every thirty days, if not more frequently. Passwords for things that are less important, such as access to entertainment Web sites that require registration, can be left unchanged for longer periods of time.

Be Extremely Skeptical of People Who Ask for Your Password

In the early days of AOL, a hacker created a program called AOHELL that allowed people to send messages that looked like they were from AOL officials. Pretending to be AOL officials, these hackers would ask random users for private information such as their passwords or credit card numbers. Once users gave up this information, the hackers could illicitly enter the users' accounts or make unauthorized charges on the users' credit cards.

While this particular type of situation rarely occurs anymore, it is still common for scammers to trick people into giving up their passwords, using various means of communication such as instant messaging, e-mail, and chat. Usually they pretend to be from a company that you have an account with, and often they will claim to be testing or repairing a program or system.

You should be wary of anyone who asks for your password. Credit card companies, ISPs, banks, and other similar institutions will never ask for your password by means of e-mail, chat, or instant messaging. In the rare event that you are required to give your password to a company, the exchange will almost invariably happen over the phone— and only when you call them.

If you are asked to give your password over the Internet, ignore the request and tell your parents right away. If your parents are not sure about what to do, have them contact your ISP.

Be Careful with Credit Card Numbers

The Internet can be a great place to shop. Often price, availability, and selection on the Internet are better than at your local shops. In Internet lingo, real world shops are called brick-and-mortar stores, and Internet shops are called e-tailers. It is true that payment for the things you buy on the Internet often can be made by mailing a check or money order to the e-tailer. Nevertheless, the most common way that consumers pay for items they purchase over the Internet is by credit card. In fact, in many cases, using a credit card is preferable to using a check or money order because of the protection against fraud that nearly all credit card companies provide.

Any time you buy something over the Internet, you should check with your parents before giving out credit card numbers. If your parents are not sure whether it is safe to submit credit card numbers to a particular Web site, suggest that they contact your ISP for more information. They may also want to check with the Federal Trade Commission and the Better Business Bureau. (For contact information, see the Where to Go for Help section at the back of this book.)

Depending on your situation, you may be allowed to use credit cards on the Internet without first getting the approval of your parents. Perhaps you have your own credit card, or maybe your parents are pretty comfortable with you using their account. (Do not assume, however, that if your parents let you use a credit card at brick-and-mortar stores without getting their permission first, that they have the same policy toward Internet shopping.)

If you are allowed to shop over the Internet without your parents' approval before each individual purchase, follow the steps below before submitting any credit card numbers.

1. Make sure that the e-tailer is using a secure shell. A secure shell prevents hackers from stealing your credit card numbers while the information is in transit between your computer and the e-tailer's server. Clues that a Web site is using a secure shell include a symbol that looks like a locked padlock (in Internet Explorer) or a symbol that looks like an unbroken key (in Netscape), usually visible in the status bar at the bottom of the browser screen. Also, for most secure sites, the URL in your browser address bar will begin with "https" instead of "http."

2. Make sure that the e-tailer is reputable. Reputable e-tailers include famous brick-and-mortar stores that have gone on-line, such as walmart.com or macys.com. Be careful, however, that you are not scammed by a company that has a name that is similar to that of a brick-and-mortar store. For instance, there may be an e-tailer called wallmart.com (spelled with two l's) that tries to confuse people looking for walmart.com. Also, be wary of Web sites that have "stolen" the domain name of a famous

company. If you are unsure about whether a Web site that looks like it belongs to a famous store actually does, call your local branch of that store and ask for its URL. There are also a handful of reputable Internet-only stores, such as Amazon.com.

3. If you are unsure about whether an e-tailer is reputable, research its background. Search for information about the e-tailer on the Better Business Bureau Web site (www.bbb.org) and on the BizRate Web site (www.bizrate.com). You can also look on USENET (accessible through www.deja.com) for comments about the company, and you can check rating sites such as ResellerRatings.com. If you are unable to locate enough information about an e-tailer, don't buy through it. Remember, if a deal seems too good to be true, it probably is. In some circumstances, deciding whether a store is reputable can take a lot of research. If after doing a reasonable amount of research, you still have questions, contact your ISP together with your parents.

4. After the transaction, report any suspicious-looking charges to your credit card immediately. Check your monthly statements (or ask your parents to do so) and make sure you know what each charge is for. If you do not want to wait until the end of the billing cycle, call your credit card company to ask about recent charges. Your credit card company may also allow you to access an on-line list of your most recent charges.

Use an Antivirus Program

There are many different types of programs or codes that can be loaded onto your computer system for malicious purposes. One of the most common is a computer virus, which is a snippet of malicious code that replicates, or copies, itself and infects multiple files within a computer. Another type is a worm, which is a self-contained program that transmits functional copies of itself to other computers (often by e-mailing itself to others using the host computer's e-mail account). This means that if a worm entered your e-mail program, it would automatically send itself to all of the e-mail addresses that you have in your account.

A Trojan horse is a program designed to make computers secretly perform a function that the computer user would not approve of. For example, in 2000, a screen saver that secretly sent AOL users' credit card information to hackers was distributed to AOL employees, who were unaware of the problem. Many people believe that viruses that do more than replicate themselves are a subcategory of Trojan horses. For the purposes of this book, we will call all of these types of malicious codes "viruses."

Computer viruses are often transmitted through files on floppy disks or through e-mail attachments. Some viruses are relatively harmless: They may play a song at random times or cause your computer to show an image. Other viruses can be extremely harmful. They may send your passwords and credit card numbers to hackers, erase data on your hard drive, or crash networks by causing hundreds of e-mails to be sent at once. In fact, some viruses can permanently damage your computer by causing it to overheat.

If you have your own computer and you use it to connect to the Internet, install an antivirus program. Many computers come with antivirus programs. If yours did not, it won't cost much to buy one. Once you have installed the program, be sure that you have enabled it and that it is scheduled to scan for viruses on a regular basis. Many programs are also capable of running in the background; if your program has this option, you should enable this, too. An antivirus program that runs in the background will protect your computer against viruses all the time. In contrast, one that does not will merely scan your computer for viruses every once in a while.

Finally, make sure your program's virus list is updated regularly. Lists containing the newest viruses should be available from the Web site of your antivirus program manufacturer, or perhaps from your computer manufacturer. Some virus programs even automatically update on a daily basis; these are particularly good. If you have any questions about your antivirus program, or if it does not seem to operate properly, contact the program manufacturer.

Install a Firewall

Firewalls are devices that stop unauthorized access to your computer while it is connected to the Internet. Firewalls can be software, hardware, or a combination of the two. Anyone who connects to the Internet should install a firewall on his or her computer. In particular, people who use a permanent Internet connection, such as DSL or a cable modem connection, should not use their connection without first installing a firewall.

20

Back Up Your Data

The previous information is intended to help you maintain your security. Even the most secure systems, however, can be cracked. To prepare for this possibility, you should regularly back up your data. Backing up your data can be as simple as saving your important documents to a floppy disk, or as complicated as installing a professional back-up program on your computer. There are also Web sites designed to back up data by saving it over the Internet. For more information about different back-up possibilities, speak to someone at your local computer store or research the possibilities over the Internet.

Protecting Your Privacy

When surfing the Net from your home, it can be hard to remember that the entire world lies behind your computer screen. As you interact in seemingly anonymous ways, you may begin to feel too comfortable giving out personal information. Ask yourself, however, whether you would give out your name and address to a complete stranger for no reason, or whether you would post a personal profile on a highway billboard for the whole world to see—of course you wouldn't! For the same reasons, you should strive to maintain your privacy when using the Internet. Behind every anonymous e-mail address and every anonymous chat room nickname lies a real person.

Maintaining your privacy means controlling how much personal identifying information you release. This includes what you submit through forms on Web sites, what you tell people who you meet in chat rooms or over instant messaging, and what you say in posts to bulletin boards and newsgroups. Every situation is different. For example, it is usually okay to give out your real name when registering for an account at a reputable Web site; in contrast, you should avoid giving out your real name to someone you meet in a chat room.

Talk to your parents to establish guidelines for what information you can and cannot give out over the Internet, and stick to these guidelines. If your parents do not fully understand a part of the Internet, demonstrate it to them on the computer and suggest that they do some research before making their decision.

Be ready to explain to your parents that the Internet may require your family to do things in new ways. For example, you might find that you are often required to provide a mailing address for activities you do over the Internet, either because you do a lot of on-line shopping or because you register with a lot of Web sites that require this information. If this is the case, your family may want to get a special P.O. Box address that you can use in place of your regular mailing address. Alternatively, your parents may ask you to use their work address instead of your home address.

What Is Personal Identifying Information?

Personal identifying information is any information that can be used to distinguish you from everybody else on the Internet. Many things can serve as personal identifying information; some of these are listed on the following page. Look through the list and think about how someone might use the information to figure out your identity.

Afterward, you may want to brainstorm with your parents for other seemingly innocent information that could in fact be identifying. Also, try to think of examples of situations where it would be okay to release a particular bit of information and some where it would not be. Personal identifying information includes:

- Your Social Security number

- Your mother's maiden name

- Your place of birth

- Your date of birth

- Your name

- Your home address

- Your telephone, cellular phone, or pager number

- Your parents' names, work addresses, and telephone numbers

- Your age

- Your sex

- Your grade

- Your school

- Your city or town

↜ Your county or state

↜ Your e-mail address

↜ Your travel plans or plans to be away from home

↜ Details about your daily routine

↜ Your teachers' or friends' names

Private information can often be accidentally released. For example, if someone's name is George Levine and his e-mail address is georgelevine@isp.com, he would be giving out his full name just by releasing his e-mail address.

You should also be careful about revealing personal identifying information about friends and family. For example, suppose you had a picture of yourself and your friends that you wanted to show to someone you met over the Internet. Even if your parents told you that you were allowed to send this picture to that person, you should get permission from the parents of the friends who also appear in the picture before sending it.

More information about how to maintain privacy while taking part in the different activities available on the Internet, such as e-mail, Web surfing, and chatting, can be found in the later chapters in this book, as well as in some of the books listed at the back of this book.

Choosing Usernames

There will be many occasions in cyberspace where you will need to choose a username. Usernames are some-times called nicknames, nicks, and monikers. On the

Internet, people are usually judged based on their usernames. For this reason, choose usernames that are gender-neutral (something not typically associated with boys rather than girls, or vice versa) and do not reveal information about yourself, such as your real name, birthday, or school.

If you need help choosing a username, flip through the dictionary and choose neutral words or a combination of neutral words, or put together random numbers and letters. Examples of good usernames include "bluejam," a combination of two neutral words, and "37mh7d9," which includes random numbers and letters. (You might find that names like the second may be slightly more difficult to remember.)

In contrast, "innocent_girl" is not a good choice for a username. It is not gender neutral and draws too much negative attention. Names that are associated with females and, in particular, young or vulnerable females, are more likely to receive unwanted attention from strangers. Also, as explained above, if someone is named George Levine in real life, then "george_levine" would not make a good username. Why? Because it reveals too much private information about the person—in this case, the person's full name.

These same guidelines for choosing usernames should be used to choose the part of an e-mail address that appears before the @ sign. Keep in mind, however, that if you choose a complicated e-mail address, such as a group of random letters and numbers, it may be difficult for your friends to remember. Your best bet would be to choose a neutral word or combination of neutral words.

In some situations, you may not be able to choose your username at first. For instance, many schools preassign usernames to their students. In these situations, if you are concerned that your username reveals too much personal information, ask your system administrator if you can change it. If you do ask, be sure to tell your system administrator why you want to change your username. Most administrators will agree to make modifications for privacy reasons.

Check Privacy Policies

Most major Web sites have privacy policies that explain what information they collect from visitors and what they do with that information. Before giving private information to a Web site, look over its privacy policy to make sure that it will not give your information to others or use it for any purpose that you don't approve of.

Some privacy policies may be written in a way that is difficult to understand. If you do not fully understand a privacy policy, ask your parents or another adult for help. If you still have questions, e-mail the Web site and ask for an explanation. In any event, if a Web site does not have a posted privacy policy, do not give it any information.

If you are under the age of thirteen, the Federal Trade Commission (FTC) requires that Web sites obtain the consent of your parents before you can give the site private information. You can find more information by visiting the FTC Web site (http://www.ftc.gov).

Disable Your Profile

If you use an instant messaging program, or if you use AOL, you should disable or blank out your profile. Also, set your program to allow instant messages only from people you know. If you use AOL, this means you should accept incoming instant messages only from people on your "buddy list" (a list that you create of people you know). These steps will reduce the chance of receiving an instant message from a stranger.

Don't Fill In Information Just Because There Is a Space for It

Many Web sites and programs provide space to fill in information but do not actually require this information. For example, some Web sites may require your full name but not your telephone number in order to register. Even so, they may provide a space for your telephone number. If the information is not required, don't bother to fill it in.

Some people even recommend filling in false information when information is required. For example, they may use a fake name or birthday to protect their privacy. While this is obviously a good way to maintain privacy, keep in mind that by giving false information, you may be violating certain contractual obligations you have to the Web site. That is, you may be going against certain terms and conditions—including a promise that you will not provide fake information—that users must agree to before they can use the Web site.

As a side note, digital signatures are special electronic signatures that verify the actual identity of a computer user. As digital signature use becomes more widespread, it may no longer be possible to register with Web sites using bogus information.

Opt Out

As you use the Internet, you will have many opportunities to protect your privacy by "opting out." For example, the majority of Web sites that require you to register will also give you the opportunity to opt out of having your information passed on to third parties. Most major advertising banner networks will let you opt out of being profiled through the use of "cookies." (Cookies are explained in chapter 4.) Most Internet "white pages" and e-mail directories will "delist" you (take you off their list) if you choose to opt out.

Because these companies make money by collecting your personal information, they will try to convince you that "opting in" is good for you. They may tell you that you will receive special offers or that you will have a better experience. Nevertheless, you should take advantage of any opportunities you are given to opt out. In the great majority of cases, the special offers will still be available even for those who choose to opt out.

Don't Be Afraid to Ask for Help

Because the Internet is so new and always changing, people have not had a chance to figure out the best way to do things. Moreover, the government has not had a chance to pass laws to protect its citizens from undesirable situations. You may find yourself in uncomfortable circumstances, or in predicaments where you are not sure about what to do. The best thing to do in these situations is to talk to a responsible adult, such as a parent or a teacher.

Sometimes when something disturbing happens, you may feel like it is your fault. You may be scared or embarrassed to talk about it with a trustworthy adult. Remember, though, that most adults understand that the Internet can take people by surprise and will not be upset with you for whatever happened. The worst thing you can do is to try to "fix" the situation yourself. Adults can also help you decide what to do and whether to contact the police or another governmental body.

You may come across people on the Internet who will try to turn you against your parents or who will try to convince you not to talk to your parents about an incident that may have happened. In fact, in some cases, people may even threaten you or someone you know with actual harm if you talk to your parents. These are the most dangerous cases. No matter what the threat is, if this happens to you, you should immediately tell your parents or another adult and have that person talk to the police. Remember, even though an intimidating message may not seem real because it appears to be coming from a computer, there is a real person at the other end of it.

Harassment

Because people can pretend to be almost anybody on the Internet, many users feel very powerful when they are on-line. High-school age boys may imagine themselves as suave, muscular college students, and girls may portray themselves as sophisticated, sexy women. While a healthy imagination is important, at times this false sense of power can lead people to cyberstalking or cyber-harassing. On-line stalking or harassment takes little more than expertise in computer usage, and almost anyone can become a cyberstalker.

You may find that you are being stalked or harassed on-line a lot more than you would be in real life. That does not, however, make it any less dangerous. Even if you think that cyberstalking is harmless—which it is not—there is always the very real danger of the stalking continuing off-line. If you think that someone may be stalking or harassing you on-line, you should tell a trustworthy adult immediately.

Use Common Sense

Keep Calm

It's easy to get excited when using the Internet. You may be bidding for a popular product or be in the midst of a heated debate with someone in a chat room or on a bulletin board. If you find yourself becoming too emotional and irrational while using the Internet, take a break to calm down. Before returning to the computer, figure out what you are trying to accomplish.

Simply Don't Respond

If you receive an e-mail, a chat comment, or a bulletin board message that is intimidating or inappropriate, or that makes you feel uncomfortable in some way, don't respond. Sending a response only encourages the person on the other end. (One common type of disturbing communication, called flaming—sending or receiving communications over the Internet that are meant as personal attacks—is discussed in detail in chapter 5.)

Your parents can help you decide if a message is particularly inappropriate; in the event that it is, you should contact your ISP and perhaps even the police. Most important, do not take the message personally. People on the Internet tend to say things that they would never say in real life. Oftentimes they will write something insulting just to get a reaction, not because they feel that you deserve it.

Educate Your Parents

It is important to talk to your parents about setting guidelines for what you are allowed to do on the Internet. Help them understand the Internet by showing them things you can do. Show them how you go about searching for your favorite band on a search engine, reading some postings on a bulletin board, and sending instant messages to your friends.

One particularly useful thing to do is to log into a teen chat room with a name like "cutie_girl." You and your parents can see the types of responses that an outgoing teenage girl might receive—and why it's important to choose your usernames carefully. You will probably receive some comments that are sexual and may be invited to a private chat area.

Stay Balanced

There is a tremendous number of things to do on the Internet. At times you may feel like you can spend hours on the computer. You may also feel like it is easier to make friends over the Internet than at school, or that the friends you make over the Internet understand you better than your off-line friends.

As engaging as the Internet can be, it is important that you do not prioritize it over your off-line life. Even if it seems to take more effort, you should make sure to maintain your relationships with your off-line friends and your family, participate in school activities and clubs, and get regular exercise.

Most important, do not neglect your studies. While the Internet can be a valuable educational tool, the most productive learning usually takes place in the classroom. Studying hard now will give you a good base of knowledge that will remain with you for the rest of your life.

Don't Believe Everything You Read

You have probably heard that, in general, you shouldn't believe everything you read. It is a particularly bad idea to believe everything you read on the Internet. You should always maintain a healthy dose of skepticism. Web sites are extremely easy to publish, and many people will publish Web sites, intentionally or accidentally, with false information. It is not uncommon for pedophiles to pretend to be teenage girls in chat rooms in order to get the attention of teenage boys.

Many scammers who want to steal your money have come up with ways of sending lies over the Internet to help them. One popular scam involves forging e-mails from a rich foreign person who needs an American bank account to hold a large sum of money. Promising a generous commission, the forger gets bank account numbers from unsuspecting victims who reply to these e-mails. Once the account numbers are turned over, the scammer will clean out these people's accounts from abroad.

Other popular scams include various "get rich quick" e-mails. These e-mails promise that you can earn large sums of money while working at home, but require an initial application fee. Needless to say, once the fees are paid, the victims never receive a penny.

Respecting Other Netizens and Staying out of Trouble

When you are anonymously using the Internet, you may feel as if you can say things that you could not say in public. Perhaps you are critical of a school policy, such as a school dress code, or perhaps you are outraged by how your local government handled a particular incident. The Internet is a great place to voice these types of concerns, and you should exercise your right to free speech—liberally and often.

On the other hand, it is important to show respect in general to other individuals on the Internet. It is easy to say hurtful or insensitive things about people when they seem like nothing more than text on your computer screen. Also, you may feel more comfortable saying such things when you are speaking anonymously.

Still, the target of your comments will be a real person—just like you—and you should exercise sensitivity. Being on-line does not excuse behavior that would be unacceptable in public. You are responsible for what you say and do, as much in cyberspace as in person.

Netiquette

The Internet community has come up with a set of guide-lines, called netiquette, to help you be a respectful neti-zen. Netiquette is always changing as new technologies are introduced; look for the latest netiquette rules on the Web. Some traditional guidelines, taken from Virginia Shea's book *Netiquette*, are detailed below. Many of these guidelines are echoed or expanded on in this book.

1. Don't say something on-line that you would not be willing to say to a person face-to-face. From behind your computer screen, it is easy to whip out insults or to be insensitive or rude. Remember, however, that there is another real person who is receiving your message.

2. Be ethical. The Internet makes things like down-loading music or copying text particularly easy. Don't steal mp3s if you believe copying music is wrong. Don't take credit for work that is not yours. Copying another person's paper is both wrong and illegal.

3. Remember that netiquette varies depending on context. While it may be appropriate to gossip about teachers when sending instant messages to classmates, it would not be appropriate to post gossip about teachers on the official school news-group. If you are unsure whether a certain com-ment is appropriate, first spend some time looking at the types of things that others are saying.

4. Remember that people have only limited time. If someone is busy, do not fill up his or her e-mail inbox with chain letters and forwarded jokes. Also, do not expect an instant response to your e-mails. Give people a chance to check their e-mail.

5. Remember that some people have slow Internet connections. Do not send them large files as attachments or direct them to Web sites that you know their connection cannot handle. If you send someone an e-mail with a large attachment, the person may have to wait for your e-mail to download before he or she can read other e-mail.

6. Write well. Use proper grammar, check your spelling, and make sure you actually know what you are talking about. Deciphering poorly written e-mails can be frustrating and time-consuming for the person receiving the e-mail. Similarly, be polite and don't swear. What you may think is an e-mail written in conversational tone may come off as rude.

7. Share knowledge. If you find an answer that you know others are looking for, or if you are an expert in a certain area, be generous with the knowledge. The Internet's greatest asset is the people who use it to communicate and share knowledge.

8. Do not make or encourage incendiary remarks (flames) in chat rooms or on bulletin boards. While flaming may be important to, and even fun

for, the people involved, it can be very annoying for the other netizens who are forced to see it.

9. Respect the privacy of others. There are many ways to do this. Below are four examples. Can you think of others?

⮫ Do not forward sensitive e-mails without first asking the original sender.

⮫ Do not pass on information about people you know or people you have met on-line without getting permission first.

⮫ If you share a computer with someone else, do not go through his or her e-mail or personal files.

⮫ Do not pry into the personal areas of public servers.

10. Do not abuse power. As you become comfortable with the Internet, you may find yourself in positions that involve a good amount of responsibility and power. Perhaps you will be asked to moderate a chat room or bulletin board, or perhaps you will be asked to administer a Web site. You should not use your position of power to manipulate people or extract favors. Treat others as you would like others to treat you.

11. Go easy on other people who make mistakes. Help new users, or "newbies," by explaining netiquette and house rules to them. If someone makes a spelling or factual error, point it out in a way that is not hurtful to the person who made the mistake.

If you have any other questions about netiquette, contact your ISP, ask an adult who would know, or consult a book or Web site on the subject (some are listed at the back of this book).

Acceptable Use Policies at School

If your school has Internet access, it probably also has an acceptable use policy (AUP). These are tailored netiquette-style guidelines that are created by your school to govern your computer use while you are there. You should find out if your school has an AUP, and if so, stick to the AUP guidelines to stay out of trouble. Know your rights as well, however. In some cases, a school's AUP may violate a student's constitutional right to free speech or to privacy. Also, with very few exceptions, a school should have no right to tell you how to use your own computer at home.

Legal Difficulties

The Internet makes many things easier to do, such as keeping in touch with friends, finding out about the weather, or researching an obscure topic. The Internet also, however, makes doing something that could get you sued easier to do. In fact, the Internet makes doing such a thing so easy that you might not even realize that you are doing it!

Two legal areas that you should watch out for are defamation and invasion of privacy. Defamation involves making untrue statements that could hurt someone's reputation. For instance, you may tell a hurtful lie about someone you know to the people in a chat room. Invasion of privacy involves taking information about someone that should be private and making that information public. Even if something about someone is true, you are not necessarily allowed to tell people—certainly not everyone who has access to the Internet!

Another legal area to be careful about is that of copyright and trademark infringement. If someone creates a work, such as a song or a story, the law gives that person the right to control in certain ways what happens to that work. These rights are called copyrights. Similarly, if a business distinguishes its products with, for instance, a special logo or shape, in certain situations the law gives the business control over how that logo or shape can be used by other people. A business' distinguishing mark, such as a logo, is called a trademark. If you download mp3s or take graphics you like from another Web site to use on your own, you may be using a copyrighted work without the author's permission. Similarly, if you are a Disney fan and you want to put the Disney logo on your personal Web site, Disney may be able to stop you from doing so because you would be using its trademark without permission.

Sending and Receiving E-Mail

E-mail is a great tool for keeping in touch with friends and family, making contact with organizations, or sending a quick note to someone. As with any form of communication, though, you must take certain precautions when sending or receiving e-mail. If you don't recognize the address to which you are sending an e-mail, for example, you have to be careful. But even if you are sending the e-mail to a close friend, there are some things you have to watch out for.

Double-Check the E-Mail Address

E-mail addresses can seem long and confusing, but the details are very important. If you mistype just one letter or number in an address, the e-mail may be sent to the wrong place. For example, an e-mail to whitehouse.gov will go to the office of the president of the United States, but an e-mail to whitehouse.com would go to a pornographic Web site! Sometimes e-mails sent to mistyped addresses "bounce back" (are returned to your e-mail account and marked as "undeliverable"), and you have little to worry about.

But sending e-mail can lead to many more errors than communicating by regular mail or telephone. For one thing, there are many more wrong e-mail addresses you could mistype than wrong numbers you could dial or wrong addresses you could send letters to. Furthermore, if you send a letter somewhere and the person the letter is addressed to does not match the address, the postal worker may not deliver it. If you dial a wrong number and do not recognize the voice of the person who picks up, you can say "Sorry, wrong number" and hang up.

In contrast, with the technology that is commonly in use today, once an e-mail to a wrong address is sent, there is no way to retrieve the e-mail or prevent it from reaching its destination. It would be like calling a wrong number but still having a conversation with a complete stranger.

Recipient Fields

Most e-mail programs have three fields in which you can specify the recipient or recipients of an e-mail: the "To" field, the "Cc" field, and the "Bcc" field. Some e-mail programs turn on the Bcc field as an option which can be turned off by default. (Look in your program documentation for more information.) Other programs do not support Bcc (or even Cc), but these are becoming increasingly rare. Cc stands for "carbon copy" and Bcc stands for "blind carbon copy." These are terms that come from the days when communications were primarily paper-based, and duplicates of letters were made using carbon paper.

The primary intended recipients of an e-mail belong in the TO field. Most e-mail programs allow multiple recipients, separated by commas or semicolons, to be entered in this field. If you want the e-mail to be received by an additional recipient to whom the e-mail is not addressed—for instance, to let your boss know that you sent another company some information—enter that recipient (in this case, your boss) in the Cc field. Below is an example:

From: daughter@isp.com
To: dad@isp.com
Cc: mom@isp.com
Subject: Soccer practice

Hi Dad!

Coach said that practice will end early today, so can you pick me up at 5:30 instead of 6:00?

Thanks!

In the example above, an e-mail is sent from a daughter to her father. Since the e-mail is addressed to her father, his e-mail address is entered in the To field. Since the e-mail is not directly intended for the daughter's mother, but she may nevertheless find the information useful, her e-mail address is entered in the Cc field.

In terms of Internet safety and privacy issues, our primary concern is with the Bcc field. Any recipient of an e-mail can see the addresses entered in the To and Cc fields. If addresses are entered in the Bcc field, however, these addresses remain invisible to everyone but the original sender of the message. The Bcc field should be used only in limited circumstances. For instance, you may wish to preserve the privacy of some of the intended recipients of an e-mail.

Kara was a high school senior applying to college. One day she received an e-mail from the admissions office of her first choice college asking for clarification about her application. After determining that the e-mail was indeed from the college and that the inquiry was appropriate, she responded to the e-mail. She wanted to let her parents see what she wrote, but she didn't think it was necessary to make her parents' e-mail address available to the college. Therefore, she entered her parents' e-mail address in the Bcc field.

The Bcc field should be used sparingly, and only when necessary. When people receive an e-mail, they assume that the visible recipients are the only recipients. Use of the Bcc field sabotages the openness and honesty that is assumed when using Internet e-mail. You can help to maintain this atmosphere by avoiding Bcc use unless absolutely necessary.

A better alternative to Bcc is to forward your sent mail to people that you would otherwise Bcc. While message recipients may assume that visible recipients—that is, those specified in the To or Cc fields—are the only recipients of a message, they do not assume that you will never forward your sent mail to anyone. (This method also avoids the danger of a Bcc'd recipient accidentally "replying to all," thereby revealing both his or her e-mail address—which you wanted to protect in the first place—and the fact that you used Bcc.) Once it is revealed that you use Bcc, people may be suspicious of any further e-mail you send them.

Kara's parents thought that her response to the college was excellent, and they replied to her e-mail to tell her so. By accident, they pressed Reply-to-all instead of Reply and their response was sent to the college as well as Kara. The college administrators shortly thereafter sent a follow-up e-mail to Kara asking who else was Bcc'd on her response. Her guidance counselor? Other college admissions offices? They also wondered whether Kara actually wrote her response herself because she seemed to be involving a lot of people.

The college administrators pointed out that they were just curious, that Kara was under no obligation to answer, and that her answer would have no effect on her admission. That following spring, however, Kara was denied admission to the college. The college explained that it was for reasons unrelated to the e-mail. Still, Kara was never sure that her e-mail had not played a role in the school's decision.

Tricks for Conveying Emotions

E-mails are quick and easy to dash off. You should keep in mind, though, that because e-mails are in writing, it is more difficult to convey emotion accurately in an e-mail than it is over the phone. Particularly troublesome is trying to show sarcasm and humor. For example, imagine someone who affectionately teases a friend by calling him a dummy. Matched with the right tone of voice, calling someone a "dummy" could be an affectionate act. Yet see how the same would look in writing:

Mike—
You dummy! You forgot our meeting this afternoon.
—Joe

In this example, Joe may not have meant to be mean to Mike, but Mike may interpret the e-mail as mean. Using sarcasm or humor in e-mails can lead to misunderstandings. One way to avoid such misunderstandings is to avoid the use of sarcasm in e-mails altogether:

Mike—
Hey, dude! You forgot our meeting this afternoon.
—Joe

But what if you prefer to keep some of your natural sarcasm and humor in your e-mails? A commonly used solution is to use emoticons. These are little symbols that you can put after a sentence to signal emotion. For instance, a smile emoticon looks like this :) or :-). (If you turn this book 90 degrees clockwise, you will see that the emoticons actually look like little smiley faces.)

If you would smile when saying something in person, then you should put a smile emoticon after you write that same thing in an e-mail. In the example above, Joe could use a smiling and winking emoticon:

Mike—
You dummy! ;) You forgot our meeting this afternoon.
—Joe

See how the comma part looks like a winking eye? Emoticons are good not only for sarcasm, but for any type of emotion that might not otherwise be adequately conveyed in plain writing. Use a sad face :(if you are sad, or use a surprised face :o if you are surprised.

More Emoticons

One alternative to emoticons is the use of several acronyms (words made up of the first letters of each word in a phrase). For instance, for funny things you can write LOL, which stands for "laughing out loud." More acronyms can be found in chapter 5.

Another alternative to emoticons is the use of emotags, which are derived from HTML. Emotags are tags that explain the emotion that goes along with the written words. To use emotags, surround the sentences in question with the emotags. Tags are made by surrounding the emotive word in brackets and using a forward slash mark in the closing tag.

I went to chemistry class today. <SARCASM> It was soooo fun. </SARCASM> I have chemistry lab this evening.

Mike didn't show up for our meeting. <ANNOY-ANCE> I can't believe he missed it.</ANNOYANCE> We'll have to reschedule.

There are a couple of other e-mail conventions you should know of. "Hahahahahaha" is a hearty laugh, "hee hee" is a giggle or a devilish laugh, <gr> is a frustrated growl, and <g> is a grin. If you use emoticons, acronyms, or emotags, be sure that the recipient is familiar with the convention. It may be helpful to explain the symbol the first time you use it:

Dad, I crashed the car! :) (That's a smiley face). Just kidding—I passed my driving test!

45

:-)	smiling
;-)	winking and smiling
B-)	smiling and wearing sunglasses
8-)	smiling and wide-eyed
:D	laughing
:-o	surprised
:-(	sad
:-P	tongue sticking out
:-J	tongue-in-cheek
:-#	sealed lips
:-&	angry
:-O	shouting
:-x	kissing
:*)	clowning around
>;->	making a devilish remark
@>+-+ —	giving a rose

Also, it is usually not a good idea to use emoticons in formal e-mails, where the e-mail would take the place of a letter or a phone call. For example, emoticons such as smiley faces should not be used in e-mails to college admissions offices or to government agencies. It is best to avoid any sort of emotionally ambiguous content in these types of e-mails.

Take a Breather

At times, you may find yourself angry or upset about something. At these times, you may feel that the best way to express your feelings is through e-mail. Perhaps you want to write to a person with whom you recently broke up because you have a few things to get off of your chest, but you are too nervous to call the person. Or perhaps you are angry with or saddened by a friend because of something that friend did. Such emotionally charged situations are not unusual.

As explained above, compared to telephone conversations or face-to-face contact, e-mail is a poor conveyor of emotions. Because of the great potential for the misinterpretation of an author's emotions, you should exercise caution before sending an emotional e-mail. Otherwise you may end up being more hurtful than you intended, or you may be wholly misunderstood.

One technique that is particularly effective is to "take a breather." Most e-mail programs allow you to save a draft of an e-mail before sending it. After you compose an emotional e-mail, instead of sending it immediately, save it as a draft. Wait twenty-four hours, then reread the e-mail and try to imagine how the recipient would perceive the e-mail. If at that point you still believe that it accurately portrays your feelings and opinions, go ahead and send it.

Sometimes things cannot wait for twenty-four hours. In this case, try to give yourself as much time as possible. What if you need to send the e-mail immediately? If you feel comfortable doing so, consider letting a neutral friend read over the e-mail on the spot.

Even if you choose not to use the "take a breather" technique when sending an emotional e-mail, you should monitor the content of your e-mail. What may be appropriate to send to a friend with whom you are angry is not necessarily appropriate to send to a teacher with whom you are angry.

Although from behind a computer screen you may feel anonymous and invincible, you are still very much responsible for the content and consequences of your e-mail. Also, keep in mind that once e-mails are sent, they cannot be retrieved. In fact, even if you delete your copy of a sent e-mail and the recipient deletes his or her copy, records of the e-mail may still remain. Mail servers are routinely backed up, and snippets of your e-mail (called packets) may be stored on random computers en route to the recipient.

Finally, you should be careful not to send anything that could be perceived as threatening. Even if you don't mean it as a threat, you could get into a lot of trouble. If you do feel like threatening or acting in a violent way toward someone, talk to a trusted adult—if not a parent, then a school counselor, a neighbor, a friend's parent, or a priest or rabbi. You will not get into trouble for having these feelings. Acting on your feelings, on the other hand, can get you into very serious trouble.

Reply to All

When replying to an e-mail that has been addressed to multiple recipients, your e-mail program may allow you to reply to just the original sender, or to everyone to whom the e-mail was originally sent. Replying to only the original author is usually accomplished with the Reply command, whereas replying to everyone is usually accomplished with the Reply to All command.

When does it make sense to use one command instead of the other? Imagine that you received an e-mail invitation to a party, and the e-mail is addressed to everyone attending the party. Unfortunately, you cannot go to the party, and you want to write an e-mail explaining why. If you knew everyone to whom the e-mail was sent, you might use the Reply to All command. In that event, everyone who received an invitation would also receive your explanation about why you cannot go. On the other hand, if you wanted to provide an explanation to only the host of the party, you would use the Reply command. In this case, your reply would be received by only the sender of the original invitation.

Be careful when using the Reply to All command. First, carefully consider whether your reply is the business of every recipient of the original message. Perhaps it makes more sense to send a reply to a subset of that group (by manually typing the addresses in the To field). Second, make sure that you recognize every single e-mail address to which the reply will be sent. Be sure to check the Cc field as well as the To field. You should do this to protect your privacy. Also, watch out that the To field does not say "undisclosed recipients"—if it does, you will not be able to reply to all of the original message recipients.

Finally, consider whether every recipient of the original message wants to receive your reply. Many people are annoyed by unsolicited e-mail and consider Reply to All replies to be in the same category as "spam," or mass unsolicited e-mails (that is, e-mails that you didn't ask to receive). It's good netiquette to avoid filling up someone's in box with extraneous material. For more information, see the netiquette guidelines in chapter 2.

A Note About Mailing Lists
A mailing list, or mail exploder, is a single e-mail address that forwards any e-mail it receives to a list of e-mail addresses. If you reply to a message from a mailing list, it may look like your reply is going to only one person because it is going to only one e-mail address. If that one e-mail address is a mailing list address, however, your reply could go to thousands of recipients. Clues to suggest that an e-mail address is actually the address of a mailing list are the words "majordomo," "listserv," "list," and "list-bot." Sometimes, though, a mailing list address is indistinguishable from a normal address. Chapter 5 of this book provides information on how to use mailing lists.

The Reply To Field
Some e-mail programs allow the user to specify one address in the From field and another in the Reply-To field. For instance, an author might choose to use an alias or forwarding address such as joe@alumni.edu while maintaining a "real" e-mail account at joe@aol.com. In this case, the author's e-mail would be from joe@aol.com, but replies to the e-mail would go to joe@alumni.edu. When replying to an e-mail, always check that the address to which you are sending the e-mail is the address of the intended recipient.

Evin's friend Noah liked to play practical jokes, some of which turned out to be quite harmful. For instance, one time Noah sent Evin an e-mail that got Evin into a fair amount of trouble.

Knowing that Evin disliked the principal at their school, Mr. Mathers, Noah sent an e-mail to Evin asking him about Mr. Mathers. This e-mail was unusual because Noah substituted his address with that of the principal in the Reply-To field of the e-mail.

From: Noah@school.edu
To: Evin@school.edu
Reply-To: Principal@school.edu
SUBJECT: Hi there
Hi there, Evin. So what do you think about our school's principal?
Your friend,
Noah

Evin quickly dashed off a reply to the e-mail.

From: Evin@school.edu
To: Principal@school.edu
SUBJECT: Re: Hi there
I hate the principal! I think he is obnoxious, annoying, and arrogant. I sincerely hope that he is fired.
—Evin

First of all, Evin should not have put such strong opinions in an e-mail, even if it was intended for only Noah to read. Noah could easily have forwarded Evin's e-mail to a number of people or posted it on a Web page. Furthermore, if the e-mail was sent from or to a school address or on a school computer, the school administrators may have had the right to look at the e-mail without Evin's or Noah's permission. Evin should have thought carefully about how to best express his strong beliefs, rather than dashing them off.

More important, however, because of Noah's little trick with the Reply-To address, Evin's reply went straight to the principal! Evin's biggest mistake was forgetting to check where the e-mail was going before sending it off.

Needless to say, Mr. Mathers was quite upset when he received Evin's e-mail. While Evin was technically allowed by law to say what he did, this e-mail did not make his time at school any easier.

Sending Mass E-Mails and Spam

Increasingly, teens are starting their own businesses. Suppose that you have a small business and would like to advertise it on the Internet. One wrong way to advertise it is to use unsolicited mass e-mails, called spam. To spam people is to send them e-mails that they did not agree or want to receive. At the time that this book is being written, the sending of spam is not illegal, but that may change soon enough.

Sending unsolicited advertisements is the worst form of spam, but spam is not limited to ads. In general, you should be wary of sending unsolicited mass e-mail. Before sending a mass e-mail, ask yourself, would all of the intended recipients of this e-mail want to receive it?

Of course, not all mass e-mails are spam. Sending a party invitation to a group of friends, even if you know that some may not be able to come, is not spam. Inviting someone to a party even if you know he or she cannot come is a nice gesture. Similarly, not all unsolicited e-mails are spam. Certainly writing to a celebrity, politician, or role model—even if your e-mail was not solicited—is one of the great things about the Internet. Even a mass unsolicited e-mail, such as an e-mail to every Fortune 100 CEO protesting corporate America's treatment of the environment, is not necessarily spam.

If you do send a mass e-mail, consider whether you want to put the recipients in the To field or the Bcc field. If you put the recipients in the To field, then the recipients can see who else received the e-mail. This may be a good idea if, for instance, you send out a party invitation to a group of mutual friends—this way, the recipients can see the other invitees. On the other hand, if the recipients of the e-mail do not know each other, or know each other only as acquaintances, you should probably put the recipients in the Bcc field. People can be sensitive about sharing their e-mail address with others, and using Bcc protects their privacy as an undisclosed recipient. (See "Recipient Fields" earlier in this chapter for more information on using the Bcc function.)

Messages with Large File Sizes

If you send a large attachment with your e-mail message and the recipients use a common e-mail technology called Post Office Protocol Version 3 (POP3), they may not be able to read their other e-mail until they have downloaded your attachment. If a recipient dials up to the

Internet with a 56K modem, your message could potentially prevent him or her from reading a time-sensitive e-mail. You should therefore avoid sending large attachments (over 200 kilobytes) unless it is necessary or unless you know that the recipient has a high-speed Internet connection. (At the very least, mention in the subject line of your e-mail that the attachment is quite large and that the person may want to wait to download it.)

If you want to send large attachments such as pictures or movies, consider making them available for download and e-mail the URL of the file rather than e-mailing the file as an attachment. There are many Web sites that will host your pictures or other files for free. At some stores, you can even choose to have your photographs scanned and posted on the Web at the same time that you have your film developed. By posting rather than attaching large files, recipients can download the media at a time that is more convenient for them.

Your E-Mail May Be Forwarded

Peter had a crush on Carlene. He had been wanting to ask her out for ages, but he couldn't get up the nerve to just walk up to her and talk to her. So he decided to send her an e-mail. He e-mailed her a love poem that he had written and asked her if she wanted to grab some coffee later that week.

Although she thought the e-mail was a little cheesy, Carlene was impressed with the poem and wanted to have coffee with Peter. Before responding, however, Carlene forwarded the e-mail to her best friend, Jenny, in order to ask what she thought.

Jenny was also impressed and told Carlene that she should go for it.

In fact, Jenny was so impressed that she forwarded the e-mail to a bunch of her girlfriends so that they could see what a great romantic Peter was. She also forwarded the e-mail to a bunch of guys at school so that they could use it as an "example."

For one reason or another, all of these people forwarded the e-mail on to more friends. . .and those friends forwarded the e-mail to their friends. By the time Peter arrived at school the next morning, practically the entire school had seen the e-mail! Peter was so embarrassed that he never spoke to Carlene again, even though she wanted to take him up on his offer for coffee.

It is important to remember that your e-mails can very easily be forwarded. Even if people have good intentions when they forward e-mail, their actions can cause embarrassment or even damage. If you have something sensitive to say to someone, consider using the phone or speaking to him or her in person. If you must communicate by e-mail, make sure the recipient is someone you can trust to keep your confidence, and ask the recipient to agree not to forward the e-mail to anyone.

Multimedia E-Mail

As systems become more advanced, it will become more common to send audio and even video e-mail messages. Audio and video messages tend to be much larger in terms of file size than text e-mails. Before sending audio or video

55

e-mails, consider whether the recipient has a fast enough connection. (Connection speed was discussed earlier.) Also, the recipient may not have the proper software to play back the message. As a courtesy, provide a link to where the recipient can download the appropriate software.

Content

E-mail is a great tool for communication, and you should feel free to use it for everything from quick notes ("Hey, Grandpa, I'm coming to visit next weekend") to semiformal letters ("Dear Sir, I am seeking employment"). Highly formal documents such as legal correspondence, however, still need to be printed on paper and sent by regular mail. Although you should feel free to use e-mail for a wide variety of functions, you should never, under any circumstances, provide the following information over e-mail:

- ⮌ Credit card numbers

- ⮌ Social Security numbers

- ⮌ Your mother's maiden name

- ⮌ Any passwords or PINs

There is no justifiable reason why anyone should require this information over e-mail. A common scam is to send an e-mail pretending to be an ISP (such as AOL) and requesting your password. Once the scammer receives the password, he or she may engage in malicious and illegal activity using your account.

You should exercise extreme caution before providing certain personal information over e-mail, such as:

➪ Your date of birth

➪ Your physical address

➪ Your telephone number

Personal information should be sent only to trusted sources, such as off-line friends or family. Before you release personal information to someone via e-mail, ask yourself, does this person really need this information? Unless the answer is clearly yes, do not send the information. If the person persists in requesting it, get your parents or another adult involved.

Receiving E-Mail

While the dangers generally associated with sending e-mail revolve around releasing private information, the dangers associated with receiving e-mail tend to revolve around being duped by fake e-mails, as well as receiving e-mail that makes you feel uncomfortable. Let's look at how to tell if an e-mail is fake.

Decoding E-Mail Headers

One way to tell if e-mails are possibly fake is to look at the headers. It is important to remember that fake e-mails can spoof (imitate) very realistic-looking headers—and that real e-mails can have suspicious-looking headers. Thus headers provide only clues, not definite answers. Also, you should rely on looking at headers only for e-mails that seem to be merely a nuisance. If you receive an e-mail that is more dangerous than a nuisance—such as a disturbing e-mail or, especially, a threatening e-mail—you should immediately tell your parents and, if necessary, your school administrators. You should also forward the e-mail to your ISP. Your ISP will let you know if you should pass on the e-mail to the police or the FBI.

The Basics

Let's play detective. When analyzing e-mail headers, the first place to look is the From field. The most obvious sign that something is fishy is if the e-mail comes from the wrong ISP. For instance, you may know that a friend of yours uses aol.com. If an e-mail claims to be authored by that friend, but comes from isp.com, that's a good reason to question its authenticity. Beyond that, however, there are several things you can watch out for. Look at the following e-mail:

> *From: tom.richards@isp.com*
> *To: you@isp.com*
> *Subject: Let's meet*
> *Hi Tina:*
> *Let's meet at the 7-11 tonight at 11:30 pm. Don't tell your parents about it! There's going to be a surprise!*
> *Your friend,*
> *Elise*

Do you notice anything strange about this e-mail? The e-mail author claims to be Elise, but it comes from the address tom.richards@isp.com! On one hand, perhaps there is a good reason for this. Perhaps Tom Richards is Elise's friend, and she was using his account. On the other hand, if there was no good reason for Elise to use Tom's account, this e-mail would be cause for suspicion.

Let's look at another example. We can leave out the message because we are interested only in the header.

> *From: Elise Robertson <tom.richards@isp.com>*
> *To: you@isp.com*
> *Subject: Let's meet*

In this case, the e-mail again appears to come from Elise. A closer look at the header, however, reveals that it still comes from the account of Tom Richards. Note that some programs, such as Microsoft Outlook Express 5, will show only a name; that is, "From: Elise Robertson," when viewing the e-mail message. In order to determine the e-mail address from which the message was sent, further action would need to be taken. Consult your e-mail program documentation for more information. Here is one final example:

> *From: Elise Robertson <elise.robertson@isp.com*
> *(unauthenticated)>*
> *To: you@isp.com*
> *Subject: Let's meet*

This header appears plausible—except for the "unauthenticated" note in the From field. The unauthenticated note usually appears when an e-mail program has sent mail using an account—in this case, elise.robertson@isp.com—but has never retrieved e-mail from that account. The importance of this is that when using the currently popular e-mail technology, a password is required to retrieve mail from an account, but no password is required to send mail from an account. In other words, anyone who properly sets up his or her program can send mail from elise.robertson@isp.com (unauthenticated), but only someone who knows Elise's password (i.e., only Elise) can retrieve mail from elise.robertson@isp.com, or send authenticated e-mail from that account.

What would a plausible header look like?

> *From: Elise Robertson <elise.robertson@isp.com>*
> *To: you@isp.com*
> *Subject: Let's meet*

Also be sure to check the To field of the e-mail. If it says "undisclosed recipients" or has a long string of names, you know that you have received a mass e-mail. Scam artists will often create e-mails to look like they are replies from friends, but looking at the To field can tip you off. Here is what a scam e-mail might look like:

> *From: 283911@isp.com*
> *To: undisclosed recipients*
> *Subject: Re: How's it going?*
> *Hey there, buddy. Let's get together soon. In the meantime, check out this great link I found:*
> *http://255.255.255.0/*
> *Your best friend—you know who I am!*

The link would send recipients to a Web page where they would be scammed or perhaps exposed to offensive material.

More Advanced Analysis

Analyzing e-mail headers can be difficult at first and will require practice. If you choose to learn the art, however, it will be an invaluable skill to staying safe on the Internet.

Most programs show by default the To and From fields. E-mails, however, contain more headers. Consult your e-mail program documentation on how to see the additional fields. The command may be located under View—>Full Headers or File—>Properties. An in-depth description of advanced header analysis is beyond the scope of this book, but some starting points are examined below. For more information, see the links listed in the back of this book.

The "X-Mailer" header describes the program used to send the e-mail. For instance, if an e-mail was sent using Microsoft Outlook Express 5, the e-mail will contain something like "X-Mailer: Microsoft Outlook Express 5.00.2314.1300."

When you are trying to determine the authenticity of an e-mail, use common sense with respect to the X-Mailer. If your friend does not use a Macintosh computer, and the X-Mailer says "X-Mailer: Claris Mailer 2.0 for Mac," you should be suspicious. Note that not all e-mails will have an X-Mailer header.

The e-mail "path" can also give you clues. For example, imagine that you receive an e-mail that claims to be from your friend who lives in Virginia. You know that your friend's ISP is AOL and yours is Mindspring.com. The e-mail has the following path shown below. Can you figure out what is happening?

Received: from mailer.stadt.nl by mailbox. mindspring.com with ESMTP id MSK38493 for you@mindspring.com; Mon, 21 Dec 2000 12:23:57 -0500 (EDT)
Received: from gateway (dialup-255.255. 255.0.Detroit2.Level3.net) by mailer.stadt.nl with ESMTP id LSK33289; Mon, 21 Dec 2000 18:20:01 (GMT)

Someone in Detroit sent the e-mail to the server mailer.stadt.nl, which sent the e-mail to mailbox. mindspring.com, where it waited to be read. Common sense should tell you that since Detroit is in Michigan, this e-mail is probably not from your friend in Virginia. Also, look at the server address: mailer.stadt.nl. It does not end in the familiar "American" endings, .com, .net, .org, .gov, .edu, or .us. It ends in .nl, which is the ending for the Netherlands. Use of a foreign domain should also raise your suspicions.

A final way to find clues is to scan the header for anything that has words such as "anonymous," "anony-mizer," and "anon-re-mailer." This is usually a flag for an anonymous re-mailer, a system that prevents an e-mail from being traced to its origin. Some people use anonymous re-mailers simply to protect their privacy, but others use them because they actually have some-thing to hide.

Internet Chain Letters, Hoaxes, and Jokes

Internet chain letters, or ICLs, are the e-mail version of traditional chain letters. Perhaps you have received an ICL that promised money or good luck. ICLs typically have three components: a hook, a threat, and a request. The hook is something used to get your attention. For example, the letter may offer ways to make money fast or to fulfill the request of a dying child. The threat usually suggests negative consequences, such as bad luck, if you break the chain. Finally, the request will ask you to do something. For example, you may be asked to mail a dollar to the last ten people listed in the e-mail, and then to add your name to the list.

Closely related to ICLs are Internet e-mail hoaxes. These are e-mails that contain false information, such as fake virus warnings, and that are intended to be forwarded. In 1994 an e-mail warning about a fictitious virus called "Good Times" was circulated. It told recipients not to open any AOL e-mail titled "Good Times." This e-mail turned out to be a hoax.

Note, however, that the "Good Times" story is indeed a plausible one. In fact, in 1999 and 2000, the "Melissa" and "ILOVEYOU" viruses were transmitted through e-mail and caused billions of dollars worth of damage. If you receive a virus warning e-mail, check reputable technology Web sites to verify that the e-mail is not a hoax. If it is not, forward the URL of the Web site containing information about the virus to people who you think should know about it. In 1997, an e-mail hoax falsely claiming to be from the founder of Microsoft was circulated. According to the hoax, anyone who forwarded the e-mail would receive $1,000. Not surprisingly, no one ever received a penny.

This is the original "Good Times" hoax:

Here is some important information. Beware of a file called Good Times. Happy Chanukah everyone, and be careful out there. There is a virus on America Online being sent by e-mail. If you get anything called "Good Times," DON'T read it or download it. It is a virus that will erase your hard drive. Forward this to all your friends. It may help them a lot.

This is the original Microsoft hoax:

From: GatesBeta@microsoft.com

Hello everyone,
Thank you for signing up for my Beta E-Mail Tracking Application, or BETA for short. My name is Bill Gates. Here at Microsoft we have just compiled an e-mail tracing program that tracks everyone to whom this message is forwarded. It does this through a unique IP (Internet Protocol) address log book database.
We are experimenting with this and need your help. Forward this to everyone you know and if it reaches 1,000 people you will receive $1,000 and a copy of Windows98 at my expense. Enjoy.
Note: Duplicate entries will not be counted. You will be notified by e-mail with further instructions once this e-mail has reached 1,000 people. Windows98 will not be shipped until it has been released to the general public.
Your friends,
Bill Gates & the Microsoft Development Team

Finally, many people enjoy forwarding jokes over e-mail. Usually these are harmless, but sometimes the jokes can be sexual or offensive. If you want to forward a joke, consider the content of the joke and to whom you are sending it. Although you may think that forwarding an off-color joke is not the same as telling it, you are responsible for everything that leaves your e-mail out box.

Be sure to remember that, even if you delete your e-mail, there is almost always a copy saved somewhere. If you forward inappropriate jokes, there could be eventual consequences, and the person bringing a claim or charge against you may have the evidence he or she needs.

In general, Internet chain letters, hoaxes, and jokes are dangerous because these electronic communications can be forwarded to huge numbers of people very easily and very quickly. This can cause systems to become clogged and can annoy recipients. At times, hoax e-mails can cause even more damage—financial damage and loss of privacy.

If you encounter an unusual type of e-mail that asks you to forward the message, talk to your parents or a trustworthy adult before you forward it. Also, consider the basic rules of netiquette (outlined in chapter 2). Would the recipients really want to receive the e-mail? Are the people to whom you plan to forward the chain e-mail appropriate recipients? As a courtesy, delete the names of people who had previously forwarded the e-mail, to protect their privacy.

If you forward the e-mail, there will be a strong possibility that millions of people will obtain your e-mail address. Your e-mail address may even be passed on to marketers or unscrupulous people. For this reason, do not use your primary e-mail account or an account that reveals your actual name to forward ICLs. Furthermore, to protect your privacy, never include your name or address in an ICL, and never participate in a "send a dollar to the people on the list" ICL.

Viruses

A relatively recent phenomenon is the transmission of computer viruses through e-mail attachments. In 1999, the "Melissa" virus, which wreaked havoc on computer systems and users, was passed between users as a Microsoft Word e-mail attachment. In 2000, the "ILOVEYOU" virus, which caused $2.5 billion worth of damage on the first day of its release, was passed between users as a Visual Basic Script attachment.

To protect yourself against viruses that are transmitted through e-mail, you should use and keep updated an antivirus program. You should download the latest updates to your applications, such as Microsoft Outlook or Microsoft Word. You should also read virus reports on a regular basis to stay informed about the latest problems. Virus reports can be found on the Web sites of antivirus program manufacturers, and at some of the sites listed at the back of this book.

There is only one way to be completely safe: If you receive an e-mail with an attachment, do not open the e-mail until you can contact the person who sent you the e-mail (either by phone or e-mail) to verify that he or she actually sent you an attachment. This may seem like a lot of work. Unfortunately, however, this is the only surefire way to protect yourself. Virus writers are becoming smarter, and earlier antivirus techniques, such as looking over the subject lines of e-mails for suspicious phrases, are becoming much less effective. For more information on how to protect yourself from viruses transmitted through e-mail attachments, contact your antivirus program manufacturer.

Threats

Remember, if you receive a threat via e-mail, or an e-mail that is harassing, offensive, inappropriate, or somehow makes you feel uncomfortable, tell a responsible adult immediately. More information is available in chapter 2.

Protect Privacy by Using Forwarding Address

A forwarding address is an e-mail address that automatically forwards all the e-mails received at that address to a designated forwarding address. The touted advantage of forwarding addresses is that they are lifelong.

Annabel began using e-mail in junior high school. By the time she was a high school senior, she e-mailed her friends more than she talked with them on the phone. She had also registered with a number of her favorite Web sites and avidly read the newsletters from those sites.

When Annabel went to college, she was assigned a new e-mail address by her school. She sent the new e-mail address to all of her friends, but some of them kept forgetting to use it, and others kept spelling it wrong. Annabel also had to reregister with many of her favorite Web sites, but she was sure that there were some that she had forgotten about. She felt like she was out of the loop, and she wanted her old e-mail address back.

Annabel realized that if she had used a forwarding e-mail address, she could have initially given the forwarding address, rather than her actual e-mail address, to her friends and family. When she went to college, she could have simply modified the forwarding address so that all of her e-mail was forwarded to her college e-mail address. That way, she could use her college e-mail account, but her friends wouldn't have had to change the address that they had on file for her. She also would have saved herself the time and energy it took to reregister at her favorite Web sites.

As you can see from the previous scenario, using a forwarding address allows you to give out one e-mail address for your entire life, even if your actual e-mail accounts change. Getting a forwarding address is as simple as choosing a new e-mail address. Just make sure that the e-mail provider offers the forwarding feature. One advantage to this is that some of those accounts will automatically filter out junk e-mail. Another advantage to forwarding addresses is that they can be used to protect your privacy. For example, if a student at Yale University enters a chat room using her real e-mail address, some_student@yale.edu, the people in the chat room would be able to figure out the student's college, and thus the student's general location. Knowing this, they might be able to get even more information, such as the student's phone number or address. On the other hand, if the same student used a forwarding address, such as some_student@forwarding.com, the people in the chat room would know much less about the student. You don't want to give away identifying information about yourself on the Internet. You should make sure to do all you can to protect your privacy on-line.

Surfing the World Wide Web

In 1989, Tim Berners-Lee, a researcher at a physics laboratory in Switzerland, began developing the system that eventually became the World Wide Web. The Web was intended to be an information space where researchers from around the world could store, retrieve, manipulate, and connect bits of scientific information. His original proposal detailed three components: the hypertext transfer protocol (http), the hypertext markup language (html), and a client called a browser. The function of "http" was to transmit information, "html" was to be used in formatting displayed information, and the browser was to be used for viewing the information.

Originally, the browser was able only to display text. In 1993, Marc Andreessen, an undergraduate at the University of Illinois, developed the first graphical browser, called Mosaic. Mosaic was an instant success because it was extremely easy to use. People only had to click on a link to access a connected page. It helped to transform the Web from a system primarily used by scientists to a popular medium. It also gave rise to the browsers used today, which can handle not only text and graphics, but audio and video as well.

Currently, the Web is based on Web pages, which are grouped into collections called Web sites. Pages across the entire system are also connected by hypertext links, sometimes called hyperlinks or links. Pages may link to, or actually include, audio and video elements, applications, and just about anything else that a computer enthusiast can dream up! "Surfing the Web" refers to moving from Web page to Web page by using links and without necessarily knowing the specific address of each page.

The best way to understand the Web and how to use it to your advantage is to spend time surfing it. A great place to start is Yahoo! (http://www.yahoo.com), a popular Web site that includes a well-maintained directory of what is available on the Web. Because the Web is like a big city, however—with great places to visit but also some shady areas—before you begin exploring, take some time to read through this chapter to learn how to stay safe while surfing.

Finding Information

There are many ways to find information on the Web. One popular way is to use a directory like Yahoo! or www.about.com. These are directories of Web sites that have been reviewed and categorized. Usually the directories are searchable, meaning that you can type in a word or phrase that you are looking for, and the directory will lead you to relevant Web sites. Sometimes the directories will recommend some sites over others. Many directories offer "teen-safe" versions that do not include pornography or other objectionable material. You should stick to these versions—don't worry, they still include all of the major games, music, and educational Web sites that are in the unfiltered version—unless you have permission from your parents to do otherwise.

Another popular way to find information is to use a search engine. Search engines send computer programs, called robots or spiders, to "crawl" around the Web and categorize what they see. When you conduct a search using a directory such as Yahoo!, you are searching the directory, which has been reviewed by humans. In contrast, when you conduct a search using a search engine, you are searching the actual content of Web pages. Because search engines, which use computer programs to index the Web, are not as smart as human beings, the results you get from a search engine tend to be less organized. Sometimes the search engine may not properly understand the context of the words on a Web page; other times, the creators of the Web page may intentionally include misleading words. Search engines are better than directories, however, for finding information on unusual topics. Because they use computers instead of humans, search engines are able to index a larger portion of the World Wide Web. A recent study estimated that the major search engines each indexed about one third of the information on the Web.

The distinction between search engines and directories is becoming blurred because the major information-finding Web sites, called portals, are combining both technologies. A third way to find information on the Internet is simply to ask. Many universities publish faculty e-mail addresses, and many professors do not mind responding to e-mail from students in search of information. Also consider posting an inquiry in a newsgroup. Before making such a post, however, learn the newsgroup safety and netiquette guidelines, which are explained in chapter 5.

Don't Believe Everything You Read

Starting from the first day of kindergarten, students are taught to learn by reading. If students want more information about something, they are used to looking for answers in textbooks, encyclopedias, newspapers, and other printed materials. In contrast, students expect that spoken information, both in the schoolyard and on the telephone, is not necessarily correct and can even include some "tall tales." Because of this difference between printed and spoken information, students tend to be skeptical of things they hear, and convinced by things they read. You may feel this way too. Are you more likely to believe something if you read it in a book than if someone tells you about it?

The Web can take advantage of this tendency to make people believe things that they otherwise would not. In the past, in order to publish a book, an author had to spend a lot of time on the book, and editors and fact checkers would review everything that the person wrote. Also, publishing a book was expensive, so publishers were not willing to risk publishing a book that contained false information. In contrast, it is very easy for a person to publish a Web page that contains wrong information, and there are usually no filters, or mechanisms, in place to combat this. And with today's Web site design programs, it is very easy for people to make the misinformation look like it comes from a large and professional Web site.

What does this mean for you? Of course, in general, it's not a good idea to assume that just because something is in a book it must be true. (After all, in the past, people have published books claiming that the world was flat, and that gold could be made from iron!) It is particularly important, however, that you do not believe everything that you read on the Web. Even though the information may be printed (either on a computer screen or from a printer), treat information on the Internet as if you would treat something you heard—not something you read in a book.

Naturally, if you had to be skeptical of everything that you came across on the Web, then it would not be a very helpful research tool or aid to learning. So there should be limits to your skepticism. If the information comes from a reputable, established Web site, you can assume that for the most part it is true.

How do you know which Web sites are reputable? For a start, if you would be willing to use a particular printed resource, such as a certain newspaper or encyclopedia, then you can assume that the Web site published by the same company is a safe bet. In other words, feel free to trust the information you come across on the *New York Times*'s Web site or *Encyclopedia Britannica*'s Web site. Government Web sites, such as the Web sites of the FDA (Food and Drug Administration) and CDC (Centers for Disease Control), can be relied upon for accurate and up-to-date information. Other established Web sites, such as CNET news (www.news.com), do not have corresponding print publications but are just as trustworthy as those that do. If you do not know whether you can trust the information on a particular Web site, ask your librarian, teacher, or parent.

Trusting a Web site does not mean putting away your thinking cap. The facts presented on a trustworthy Web site are probably true; however, you should feel entitled to disagree with the opinions, and in some cases you are obligated to disagree with them.

If you surf the Web frequently, at some point you may come across facts that you know are just plain wrong, as well as opinions that are sickening to you or seem even downright evil. For instance, you may come across Web sites that promote the hatred of, or discrimination against, people of a certain ethnicity, gender, religion, or sexual orientation. Out of all the sites that exist on the Web, there are probably many that contain information or opinions that you would find inappropriate, offensive, or even frightening.

Web Sites to Avoid

There are some Web sites you should avoid, no matter what. These include:

➭ Web sites that contain pornographic material, including written, graphic, and aural (heard) material. Web sites that appeal to the sexual or the excretory interests of people are definitely to be avoided. In contrast, Web sites that offer educational material relating to sex, such as how to have safe sex or information about sexual orientation, may be appropriate for you to look at. Check with your parents first—the rules are different in every family.

➭ Web sites that promote the hatred of a particular ethnicity, gender, religion, or sexual orientation. This includes white supremacy and antigay sites, such as those of the Ku Klux Klan. It may, however, be useful to visit these types of sites to learn about why the opinions of these groups are harmful. If you do visit this type of site, be sure to do so in the company of a trustworthy adult, such as a teacher, librarian, or parent. Have them explain in detail why the opinions you come across on the site are dangerous. If you don't understand, ask questions until you do.

➭ Web sites that promote illegal, violent, or dangerous activities. Web sites dedicated to activities such as building pipe bombs can falsely convince you that building bombs is easy and is not dangerous. Remember, oftentimes information posted on Web sites is just plain wrong.

➭ Web sites that promote the use of drugs, including alcohol and tobacco. It is illegal for minors (anyone under eighteen) to consume alcohol or use tobacco, and it is illegal for anybody, with very few exceptions, to use recreational drugs such as marijuana and LSD. If you want more information about how drugs or alcohol affect your body, visit your local library or the many excellent drug abuse prevention sites on the Web.

↩ Any Web site that you find offensive, intimidating, or inappropriate, or that makes you somehow uncomfortable. The Internet is available for your benefit. In general, you are not required to go to any Web site that you do not want to. If you think, however, that you should visit a Web site that makes you feel uncomfortable—for example, you may feel that it is important for you to see a Web site about torture and international human rights violations, even though some of the images bother you—ask a trustworthy adult to sit with you.

If you come across a Web site that you think you should avoid, press the Back button on your browser. In most cases, this should return you to a safety zone. If you find that you are "trapped" by the Web page—that is, if the Back button has no effect—press the Home button located on your browser. Finally, if windows keep popping up and you are unable to get rid of them, or if the methods described above do not seem to work, turn off and restart the computer.

Jasper was surfing his favorite computer game Web site when he noticed a link posted by another user of the site, promising screen shots of the sequel to his favorite game. When he clicked on the link, however, he arrived at a pornographic Web site. Jasper clicked the Back button, but it didn't take him back, and windows with pornographic pictures started popping up all over his screen.

Jasper didn't know what to do. He wanted to ask his father for help, but he was too embarrassed. He was worried that his father would think he was looking at pornography.

Finally, he decided that he had to ask his dad for help. His father tried to close all of the windows, but more kept popping up. So together they restarted the computer, which made the problem finally go away.

"Dad," Jasper said, "I want you to know that I wasn't looking at dirty Web sites. Seriously. I don't do that kind of thing."

"Don't worry, Jasper," his father replied. "I've read that these kinds of things happen to a lot of people on the Internet. You should come talk to me about any type of problem you're having."

Whenever you are using the Internet, if you need help or have questions, you should feel comfortable going to a trustworthy adult. Most adults know that the Internet is a place where strange things can happen.

Using Filters

The Internet contains both good and bad content, and the amount of content is too overwhelming for any one person to evaluate all of it. In order to keep bad content out of their computers, people use a technology called filtering. When someone requests a Web page using a system that has filtering technology, the filtering program evaluates the request. If the program determines that the requested page contains acceptable content, it displays the page to the user. If the program determines otherwise, it does not.

Filters can operate at many levels. The Chinese government currently filters Web pages for all of China. Some schools filter Web pages for every computer on the school network. The most common application of filters, however, is for individuals to use on their personal computers.

Filters use a variety of technologies. Keyword filtering involves filtering Web pages that contain certain keywords, such as "sex." An offshoot of keyword filtering is filtering technologies that evaluate images for flesh tones, or colors that resemble human flesh. (These technologies look for nudity.) Restricted site filtering involves filtering URLs based on a list compiled by a third party, such as a filtering software manufacturer or an organization with a specific set of beliefs. The Platform for Internet Content filtering system involves making Web sites rate their own content based on different categories.

As you have probably guessed, no existing filtering technology works perfectly. There will always be some objectionable material that can slip through any system, and there will always be acceptable material that may be accidentally filtered. Furthermore, filtering systems that use third party restricted site lists may filter according to beliefs that are different than yours or your parents'. On the other hand, using filters is a convenient way to stay generally safe on the Net. Talk to your parents about the pros and cons of filtering to decide if it is appropriate for your situation.

Protecting Your Privacy

When you simply surf the Web—without filling out any forms—you may think that you are doing so without giving any information to the Web sites that you visit. In fact, however, the opposite is true. Every time you look at a Web page in your browser, you are giving the host of the Web site certain information.

HTTP Header Information

Every time a browser requests a page from a Web site, it sends information through something called an http header to the Web site host computer, called a Web server. Following are examples of some of the information that is revealed.

The Browser and Version You Are Using

If you are using a standard browser, such as Netscape Communicator 4.5 or Microsoft Internet Explorer 5.1, every Web site that you visit will be given the name and version of the browser. Generally, this information cannot be hidden. However, special "middlemen" called proxy servers can be set up to hide this information by putting garbage in the part of the http header where the browser information normally goes. You may also be able to download a "patch" for your browser that does the same thing.

The Link You Just Came From

If you arrive at a page by clicking a link on another Web page, the address of the first Web page is given to the second. This is called the referring link.

Suppose, for example, that you are reading a story on CNN located at http://www.cnn.com/story.html. Within that story, there is a link to the White House Web site, at http://www.whitehouse.gov. If you click on that link, the White House Web server will be told by your browser that you just came from http://www.cnn.com/story.html.

One way to avoid revealing this information is to type the URL directly in the browser address bar. So in the example above, rather than clicking on the link, you could type http://www.whitehouse.gov directly into your browser. If you do that, the White House will not know what Web page you were previously visiting.

Your Internet Protocol Address

Every computer that is being used to surf the Web has associated with it a unique Internet protocol address, or IP address. This address is in the form of a string of numbers, such as 127.0.0.0. Typically, when you access a Web page, you send your IP address to the Web site in the http header.

Blocks of IP addresses are assigned to different ISPs, much like blocks of houses belong to different cities. If you access a Web page, the Web site that hosts that page can determine the identity of your Internet service provider. This is done through a process called reverse-IP lookup. This capability exists only if you use an ISP to connect to the Internet, but nearly everybody does. In other words, if you connect to the Internet using AOL, then every Web site you visit will know you are using AOL.

If you have a permanent Internet connection, then every Web site you visit may be able to easily determine the exact computer you used to connect to the Internet. If your computer has a name, like many school workstations and servers do, then every Web site you visit will know the name of your computer as well.

On the other hand, if you connect to the Internet using a modem and a phone line, then you will most likely use a system that gives you a different IP address every time you access the Internet. In other words, your IP address will constantly change, and Web sites will have a hard time associating an IP address with a particular computer.

Finally, many ISPs use something called a proxy server to go between their subscribers and the Internet. If the proxy server is set up in a particular way, Web sites will see the IP address of the proxy server rather than that of the user.

While dynamic IP addresses and proxy servers can protect your privacy to some extent, ISPs keep the types of records necessary for people to figure out exactly which computers accessed which Web sites at a particular date and time. If a Web site files a lawsuit against you, or if the government thinks you have committed a crime, the ISP will most likely have to release any relevant information.

Cookies
Cookies are little bits of text that Web sites place on your hard drive. Every time you access a Web site that has

given you a cookie, you send a copy of the cookie back to the Web site through the http header.

> Manu was visiting his favorite Web site, asdf.com. He came across a form on the Web site asking him to register his name and e-mail address. Manu asked his parents for permission to register. After looking over the Web site's privacy policy, Manu's parents agreed that he could register.
>
> Once Manu had submitted the registration form, asdf.com put Manu's information in its database and assigned an identification number to Manu. The site then packaged Manu's ID number into a cookie, and sent the cookie to be stored on Manu's hard drive.
>
> The next time Manu visited asdf.com, his browser automatically sent the cookie to asdf.com. When asdf.com received the cookie, it was able to tell that Manu's computer—and not that of another person—was visiting its site, and asdf.com was able to make him a special home page. Instead of the usual asdf.com home page, Manu saw one that said "Welcome Manu" and had special messages just for him.

Cookies can be sent back only to the Web site that put them on your hard drive in the first place. In other words, if Amazon.com put a cookie containing your name onto your hard drive, BarnesandNoble.com could not somehow "grab" this cookie to figure out your name. Also, notice that by design, cookies can contain only information that you gave out in the first place. An

Amazon.com cookie cannot retrieve information directly from your computer; you must have given information to Amazon.com at some point in order for that information to be in your cookie.

At the moment, however, advertising banners are creating a privacy problem. Advertising banners are the usually rectangular graphics that often appear on the top of Web pages. These graphics usually advertise a product or service and can be clicked on in order to learn more about what is being advertised.

In the above example, if Amazon.com and BarnesandNoble.com used the same ad banner company, that company could serve as a "bridge" between the two Web sites. In this case, BarnesandNoble.com would be able to grab information you gave to Amazon.com by using the ad banner as the middleman.

If you are uncomfortable with this possibility, you can turn off cookies in your browser preferences. Unfortunately, cookies are used for many common on-line tasks, such as on-line shopping, and if you turn them off you may find yourself limited in what you can do on-line. Another possibility would be to "opt out" of ad banner profiling systems. Most major advertising banner companies provide a way to do this on their Web sites. If you do opt out, don't forget to re-opt out if you install a new browser or switch to a different browser.

Using Public Computers

In the section above, you saw how a substantial amount of personal information can "leak out" of your browser, even if you are using your own computer. If you use a public computer, such as one in a school or a library, to surf the Web, there are other places where information about your browsing habits can be discovered.

There are five major ways that current major browsers can reveal information about your browsing habits:

1. History list. The major browsers keep a "history list" that lists the URLs of every single Web page recently visited, as well as the time and date of the visit.

2. Cache. The browser cache is an area where copies of recently visited Web pages are stored. If someone looks through the cache after you have surfed the Web, they will be able to see the graphics and text of pages you recently visited.

3. Cookies. If someone were to look through the cookies list, which contains the time, date, and Web site of each cookie, he or she would be able to figure out which sites you had visited (provided that those sites used cookies). Most major Web sites use cookies.

4. Browser address bar. The browser address bar is the area at the top of the browser where you type in a URL, such as http://www.pbs.org. When you pull down the address bar, you can see URLs that have been recently typed into the browser. Furthermore, the browser will automatically fill in the rest of a URL name when someone begins typing it in the address bar, provided that the browser had previously accessed that URL. So, for

example, if you typed www.hotm, the address bar would automatically fill in the rest of the address to make it www.hotmail.com.

5. The Back button. If you walk away from a computer without first closing the browser, the next user can press the Back button on the browser to see all of the Web sites that you just visited.

If you use a public computer, protect yourself by clearing the history list and the cache, deleting the cookies, and shutting down the browser before you leave the computer.

Filling Out Forms

The most common way that people interact with Web sites is by filling out forms. Filling out forms can involve something as simple as typing a search term into a search engine, or something as complex as opening up a bank account on-line. You may be asked to fill out a form with personal information when registering for a chat room or entering a contest. If you do any shopping on-line, you will probably need to provide information such as your shipping address and your credit card number.

As discussed in chapter 2, to be safe, you and your parents should first check to see if the Web site has a privacy policy, and if it does, what the Web site does with your personal information. In particular, if the Web site uses your personal information for anything more than the immediate transaction or registration, you should avoid giving out this information. If you are confused by the privacy policy after reading it, or if you cannot find a privacy policy, send an e-mail to the site requesting a policy statement before you release personal information. You may also wish to contact your ISP for help.

Opting Out and De-Registering from Web Sites

If you register with a Web site, you may be given the opportunity to receive special offers or to be entered into a contest. In exchange, you will be asked to allow your personal information to be used by other companies. In general, you should avoid these opportunities. Once your personal information is placed on general marketing lists, it is usually very difficult to remove. You could expose you and your family to junk mail, spam, and telemarketing calls.

At times you may also want to de-register from a Web site with which you had previously registered. Perhaps the Web site sends you too many e-mails, or perhaps you simply no longer wish to visit the site. De-registering from a site usually involves e-mailing the site Web master with the request. Below is a sample e-mail:

To: webmaster@a-website.com
Dear Webmaster:
I no longer wish to be registered with your Web site. Please remove completely any personal information of mine, including my name, address, telephone number, and e-mail address from any property in which you have stored, either permanently or temporarily, that information, including your Web site, database, and mailing lists. Please also ensure that my information is removed from any affiliated or

third party properties in which you directly or indi-rectly, fully or partially, permanently or temporarily, or otherwise, caused my personal information to be stored. Thank you in advance.

If you believe that, even after de-registering, a Web site is retaining some of your personal information, ask your parents to contact your ISP for help.

On-line Shopping

On-line shopping—also known as e-commerce—can be fun and convenient. Eighteen percent of people who use the Internet make purchases on-line, and that number is expected to grow tremendously in the next few years. Almost anything, from Christmas trees to prescription medicines, can be purchased on-line.

If you decide to purchase something on-line, double-check that you have permission from your parents. If you submit credit card information to an on-line store, make sure that the e-tailer is reputable and that it uses a secure connection (see chapter 2 for more information). In 1999, over $400 million worth of fraudulent on-line purchases were made using credit cards. If your family does a lot of cybershopping, your parents may want to get a special credit card just for on-line purchases.

If you or your parents suspect that your credit card numbers have been stolen, contact your credit card com-pany immediately. You are liable only for up to $50 worth of fraudulent purchases, but you must carefully monitor the use of your credit card numbers.

On-line Auctions

A popular way for businesses to sell items on-line is through auctions. In an auction, buyers compete against each other for a product by bidding higher and higher amounts that they are willing to pay. The auction has an ending time, and whoever bids the highest amount before the auction ends is entitled to purchase the product. Some auctions award products to a number of top bidders. For example, ten computers may be auctioned at once to the ten highest bidders. If an auction has a reserve price, the seller is not obligated to sell the product unless the highest bid meets or exceeds the reserve price. Usually, the buyer is also not obligated to buy the product unless the reserve price is met.

On-line auctions can be a lot of fun and can be a great way to buy things for less than you would have to pay at a regular store. Ask your parents for permission before you participate in an on-line auction; do not assume that if you have permission to shop on-line that you also have permission to bid on auctions. Also, if you are under eighteen, check with the site to see if it allows minors to participate.

If you are allowed to participate, you need to follow two very important rules. First, make sure you fully understand the rules of the auction site. If you win an auction, you are usually required to purchase the product being auctioned. If you renege (go back) on a commitment to buy something in an auction, you could actually be sued! For this reason, it is very important that you understand the auction rules before bidding. You don't want to wind up in a situation where you won an auction, but you think you lost the auction, or you think you won it, but for a different price. And don't assume that the conventions of one auction site apply to another; each site has different rules about winning bids, extending auctions past their ending times, reserve prices, transaction fees, and other matters.

Second, set a final limit in your head before you place your first bid and stick to it. Bidding for a product can become very exciting, especially during the period of time right before the auction closes. People will try to place the highest bid at the last second so that their competitors don't have the opportunity to outbid them. You can get lost in the excitement and end up bidding much more for a product than you originally wanted to pay. If the bidding exceeds the final limit you set for yourself, you may begin to think that if other people are willing to pay more, then you set your limit too low. Avoid this temptation by knowing that the other bidders are probably thinking the same thing that you are thinking. In terms of what a product is really worth, it may be a case of the blind leading the blind.

Person-to-Person Auctions

A special type of auction is the person-to-person auction. These auctions differ from e-tailer auctions because the seller is typically not a business, but a regular person. You may have heard of eBay, probably the most famous person-to-person auction Web site.

Most person-to-person auction Web sites require their users to be at least eighteen years old. If you want to bid for an item or product on one of these sites and you are under eighteen, ask your parents to do the bidding for you. As is the case with regular auctions, in person-to-person auctions, the bidder should know the auction site rules and set a final limit in his or her head before bidding.

Because every seller in a person-to-person auction is different, experiences can vary dramatically—even when using the same Web site every time! That is why it is important for the bidder to be extra careful about guarding against fraud. He or she should look at the seller's feedback to determine the person's reliability as a seller in the past, and look for possible hidden problems with the product. This means carefully going over all of the terms of the auction, such as the shipping and tax terms, and e-mailing the seller with any questions before the first bid is placed.

Once an auction is won, if the auction item is worth a lot of money, you may want to consider using an escrow service. These services, such as I-escrow.com, will withhold your payment from the seller until you have had a chance to inspect the item. In any event, carefully document the entire auction transaction, and verify in writing (e-mail) any agreements that may have been made over the phone or through instant messaging.

Downloading Files

There are many ways for you to receive files. They can be e-mailed to you as attachments, sent to you using an instant messaging program, or posted to newsgroups. As new technologies are invented, there will probably be even more ways to transfer files.

Currently, the most common way to download a file is to follow a link on a Web page. Once you do so, the file may be downloaded using a protocol called file transfer protocol (FTP), or the familiar http.

You should download files only from sources that you trust. Sometimes downloadable files from shady sources turn out to have viruses or other malicious programs hidden in them.

If you plan on downloading a file, make sure you know which directory on your computer the file will be saved to. Once a file is finished downloading, scan it with up-to-date antivirus software to be sure that it is clean. If you download a program that needs to be installed and you share your computer, before installing the program, alert anybody who may be affected and check whether the installation poses any problems for them.

Chat Rooms, Newsgroups, and Mailing Lists

Chat rooms are places on the Internet where you can have a live "conversation" with others who are on-line at the same time. Everything you type can be seen by others who are in the same chat room. Newer chat room technologies allow people to send live audio and even video, in addition to typed text.

The original chat rooms on the Internet use a system based on Internet Relay Chat (IRC) and are connected by special servers across the world. On IRC, you can find a chat room in just about any language, dedicated to just about any topic. Popular Web sites, including some aimed at teens, may also have their own chat rooms. Unlike an IRC chat room, which is open to the entire world, a chat room of this type is generally restricted to people who enter the room through its Web site.

Chat rooms can be centered on a variety of topics, from politics to computer programming. Not all chat rooms are focused on fun or harmless topics, however. You may come across chat rooms that are organized around topics such as cults, sex, violence, and intolerance. Even if you do not take the topic very seriously, others in the chat room might. They may want to engage in some of the activities about which they chat, and they may want to involve you as well.

Most chat rooms are open. This means people can say whatever they want in the room, although there may still be a discussion leader who tries to keep chatters on topic. Some chat rooms are moderated. In a moderated chat room, the moderator can "kick out" chatters if they say inappropriate things. In some strictly moderated chat rooms, chatters must send all of their messages to the moderator, who then decides whether to permit the messages to be said.

Private chat rooms are rooms where chatters may invite others to have private conversations. If a private chat room is "listed," others may barge into the room.

Chat Room Netiquette

Chat rooms are full of netiquette rules. Some of these rules are consistent across chat rooms. For example, typing in all capital letters is thought of as shouting, which is considered rude. Other rules are specific to particular chat rooms. Some rooms may ask you to read a Frequently Asked Questions (FAQs) document before entering the room. Other rooms may require you to stay strictly on topic.

If you are unfamiliar with a chat room, spend some time observing when you first enter. After you feel more comfortable, say hello to the room. Don't become upset if no one immediately begins talking to you—treat the experience like a party full of interesting people, and try to add something to the conversation.

Common Chat Room Acronyms

AFAIK As far as I know
AFK Away from keyboard
BAK Back at keyboard
BTW By the way
CYAL8TR See you all later
FYI For your information
GFETE Grinning from ear to ear
GMTA Great minds think alike
IMHO In my humble opinion
IOW In other words
IRL In real life
LOL Laughing out loud
LMAO Laughing my ascii off
MYOB Mind your own business
OTOH On the other hand
POV Point of view
ROFL Rolling on the floor laughing
THX Thanks
YGIAGAM Your guess is as good as mine

<bg> Big grin
<g> Grin
<s> Sigh
<vbg> Very big grin

Chat Room Safety

Lisa's parents bought a new computer that came with America Online (AOL). Lisa enjoyed using the computer and spent many hours e-mailing her grandmother and instant messaging her friends. Lisa also enjoyed randomly surfing around AOL.

One day, she came across the AOL chat rooms. As soon as she entered a room, someone named "fun_dude" struck up a conversation with her. Somehow, fun_dude seemed to understand her better than anyone else she had ever met. They chatted late into the night.

Lisa began chatting with fun_dude more and more often. She would usually log on after school and chat until dinnertime. Sometimes Lisa would chat some more after dinner. Her friendship with fun_dude became increasingly intimate; at one point, fun_dude asked for her phone number. Even though Lisa should have checked with her parents first, she went ahead and gave it to him. She thought that perhaps she was in love.

The next afternoon, the phone rang. It was fun_dude.

"Lisa, this is fun_dude. I really want to meet you."

"Umm, I don't know if I should . . ." Lisa said.

"C'mon, we're such good friends," fun_dude exclaimed, "and we'll be even better friends if we meet in person."

Fun_dude eventually put enough pressure on Lisa that she agreed to meet him. He told her that they should meet in the parking lot of Lisa's school at 9 PM. "No one will be there," fun_dude explained, "so we'll be able to talk without being interrupted."

Lisa went to the school parking lot that night. She felt weird because the parking lot was completely deserted except for one parked car. As she headed toward the car, she saw fun_dude emerge from the woods behind the parking lot. He was smoking a cigarette and looked nearly forty years old! This was not at all how Lisa had imagined him. Fortunately, fun_dude hadn't seen Lisa, so she quickly turned around and went home. She had difficulty sleeping that night.

The next morning, Lisa's e-mail in box was filled with messages from fun_dude. He sounded angry with her. Lisa then did what she should have done a long time ago: She told her parents everything that had happened. They then discussed whether they should contact the police. Lisa was told to ignore fun_dude's messages.

After a few weeks he stopped e-mailing, but Lisa and her family remained concerned. Eventually, they changed their phone number, and Lisa vowed never again to enter a chat room—or to give out any personal information over the Internet.

Chat rooms can be fun places to hang out. But they can also be one of the most dangerous places on the Internet. For this reason, we recommend that you do not participate in chat rooms without a parent or a responsible adult by your side. Following are a few important additional pieces of advice about chat rooms.

1. Remember that people are not always who they appear to be. Many people log on to chat rooms because they want to "try on" new identities. Old men may want to try being young girls. Teenage boys may want to be college athletes. Other times, people may take on the identity that best allows them to take advantage of other people.

2. Don't ever feel trapped. Remember that when you enter a chat room, you should stay in control. You should never feel trapped in a private chat room with someone, or trapped into revealing information about yourself. If you find yourself feeling overwhelmed by a chat room, tell yourself that you can always turn off the computer.

3. Choose a chat room nickname that is gender-neutral and does not reveal your location or identity. In other words, do not choose a name that is a typical "boy" or "girl" name. Also, do not choose a name that contains information about your location, such as your town, school, or county. Also, do not choose a nickname that reveals your real name in any way. If someone's real name is Daniel Fitzpatrick, that person should not use chat room names like "DashingDan" or "d_fitzpatrick." If you use AOL, use two different screen names, one for e-mail and one for chat. For more information about choosing usernames, see chapter 2.

4. Do not give out personal information to "friends" you make in chat rooms. It is true that some

people have met in person and become friends with people they first met in chat rooms. In fact, some people have even married people who they met in chat rooms. Stories like these, however, are unusual. In general, chat room friends should not be confused with off-line friends. Why? Because it is much harder to trust the people you meet in chat rooms to really be who they say they are. For this reason, you should never give personal information to a friend you make through a chat room. This includes giving out your

➮ Real name

➮ E-mail address

➮ Telephone number

➮ Home address

➮ School address

Also, don't reveal any other information that someone could use to figure out your real identity. By the same token, respect the privacy of others, and don't ask them for personal information.

Meeting a Chat Room Acquaintance in the Real World

Ideally, you should never meet a chat room "friend" in real life. If, despite this advice, you still plan to meet someone, bring a parent or other adult along, and meet in a public place such as a mall. It is best if beforehand your parent speaks on the telephone with the parent of the person you want to meet. Be very suspicious of someone who tries to discourage you from involving your parents in the meeting.

Newsgroups

Newsgroups, sometimes called bulletin boards or forums, are places to share information on a specific topic. Topics can include anything from local politics to a popular band. Newsgroups are different from chat rooms because the communications do not take place instantaneously; they are instead "posted" to a news server. Like chat rooms, newsgroups may also be moderated. The moderator may delete offending posts, or posts may have to be cleared by moderators before they are able to be seen by newsgroup users.

The original Internet newsgroups are part of something called USENET. Like IRC, these newsgroups are hosted on special servers and are open to anyone in the world. USENET newsgroups start with prefixes like "alt." or "rec." Although USENET postings eventually expire (disappear), they are still archived by Web sites such as Deja.com. On Deja, newsgroup postings are also searchable. That means for years after you post something to a newsgroup, long after the post officially expires, people will be able to look up your post. Keep this in mind before you post something.

Web sites may also have their own newsgroups or forums apart from USENET, just as they have their own chat rooms apart from IRC.

Programs that are used to post to newsgroups by default expose your name and e-mail address. Using your real e-mail address with newsgroups can cause you to reveal private information as well as to have your e-mail address put on spam lists. If you are on a spam list, you will receive a substantial amount of unsolicited e-mail. In order to avoid this, configure your newsreader to use a bogus name and e-mail address.

The same guidelines that apply to staying safe in chat rooms apply to newsgroups. In addition to your real name and e-mail address, never reveal information such as your telephone number, home address, and school address. For more on what personal information you should avoid revealing, see chapter 2.

Newsgroups exist for almost any topic under the sun. Stay away from newsgroups that have titles indicating that they contain sexual, violent, or offensive content, or any other type of topic that may make you feel uncomfortable. If you come across this type of content, talk to a trustworthy adult about it. You may even want to report obscene content to your ISP.

Mailing Lists

Mailing lists can be thought of as newsgroups that take place over e-mail. With a mailing list, however, instead of posting your comments to a newsgroup, you send an e-mail to a special address. This special address then forwards your e-mail to everybody else subscribed to the mailing list. Schools, local clubs, and organizations commonly use mailing lists.

Because by definition you must provide your e-mail address when joining a mailing list, ask your parents for permission before you join one. Think about using an e-mail forwarding address to make it difficult for other subscribers to determine your real address. Also, configure your e-mail program to use a nickname instead of your real name.

Precautions similar to those taken with chat rooms and newsgroups should be taken with mailing lists. In addition, there are some special netiquette rules that apply to mailing lists:

- ↩ Keep your messages brief and on topic, and try to combine multiple responses into one message. If you quote someone else, delete all parts of his or her e-mail except the relevant portions. This keeps the amount of e-mail traffic, which can be overwhelming with large mailing lists, to a minimum.

- ↩ Refrain from sending large attachments. Some users may have slow Internet connections, and downloading large attachments may be considered by them to be a nuisance.

- ↩ Avoid sending messages that do not add to the conversation. An example of such a message would be an e-mail that simply says "I agree!" This does little more than add to the amount of e-mail traffic.

- ↩ Have a clear opening and closing to your message, and identify yourself with a consistent nickname.

102

⌐ Be patient with people who are new to the list and do not understand its intricacies. Everyone is a "newbie"—someone new to the system—at some point.

Responding to Flames

If you spend time in chat rooms, on bulletin boards, or on mailing lists, you will soon learn about "flaming." Flaming is the act of writing something for the purpose of inciting anger. Consider the following hypothetical mailing list exchange:

Yan: Britney Spears rules my world. I love all of her music and think that she is beautiful.

Peter: Britney Spears is the worst singer in history. She has no talent, and I suspect that she is tone-deaf.

Mike: Yan, you are a total loser. You should be banned from this mailing list solely on the basis of your stupidity.

In this example, the postings of both Peter and Mike made Yan very angry. But there is an important difference between the two responses. Peter's response is on topic and addresses only Yan's opinions, not Yan himself. If you are having a strong disagreement with someone, you should follow Peter's lead and remember always to stay on topic and to attack opinions and not people.

Mike, on the other hand, is flaming Yan. Mike's post is off topic because it makes no mention of Britney

Spears. Furthermore, instead of attacking Yan's opinions, Mike attacks Yan himself. Although Mike suggests that Yan should be banned, if the above exchange actually took place, most mailing list Webmasters and netizens would actually want to ban Mike!

You may find yourself being flamed from time to time. If you receive a flame, the best thing to do is not to respond to it. Remember, people flame to incite anger. If the flamer doesn't know that he or she has made you angry, he or she will feel stupid and probably stop.

If you feel that you must respond to a flame, remember to keep your response on topic and to attack opinions, not people. Be sure to include in your response that you oppose being flamed and will not participate further in discussions with people who do it. You may also wish to contact the flamer's ISP, parents, and school administrators (if applicable).

Finally, note that there is a big difference between a flame and a threat. If you receive an e-mail, chat message, newsgroup posting, or other form of on-line communication that is threatening or that you perceive to be threatening, you must immediately tell your parents, your school administrators and teachers (if applicable), and even the police. Threats made over the Internet must not be taken lightly, and if you are unsure about whether something is a threat, ask an adult about it immediately. Several students lost their lives and many more were injured in a school shooting at Columbine High School in Colorado in 1999, partly because a threatening Web page was not taken seriously. School officials are now taking such things much more seriously.

For your purposes, consider a threat to be anything that makes you feel uncomfortable or worried that you may be physically harmed. For example, receiving a pornographic picture of someone who is or looks like a minor is something you should consider to be very threatening.

Publishing on the Web

Web pages are quite easy to publish. Maybe you know people who have their own Web sites, or perhaps you have even published your own! Web sites are most commonly made up of text and images. The text and formatting information is written in HTML. Web sites may also have other components, such as videos, music, or chat rooms.

There are many different ways to create Web sites. You can learn HTML or use a program called an HTML editor to help you. You can even just point-and-click on other Web sites that will help you create your own. Let's look at some important information that you should know if you decide to publish your own Web site.

Protect Your Privacy

Generally, pages on the Web can be accessed by anyone. This means if you put up a Web page, anyone—including creeps, criminals, and con artists—can view your page. For this reason, if you choose to publish a site, you should avoid putting up personal information that can be used to help identify you. When publishing a Web page—especially the first time—it can be easy to get carried away, go against common sense, and put everything about yourself on the Web page. Don't let this happen!

If visitors to your site need this type of information, they can e-mail you—that keeps you in control over who gets this information. Before sending e-mails with this type of information, get permission from your parents. You should also avoid publishing information such as photos of yourself, your family, or friends, or the location or name of the town or city you live in (if it is small).

Instead of photographs of yourself or your friends, consider publishing photos of your pet or favorite object. If you absolutely must publish a photograph of yourself, get permission from your parents first. Also, always check with your friends and family before publishing photos of them, and if they are under eighteen, make sure you get their parents' permission. If you do get permission, show the published page to whomever is featured in it and confirm that you still have permission (or if applicable, parental permission).

So if you can't publish pictures of your friends, what can you publish? Web pages are good places to publish things like your favorite food, poem, or cartoon character; the names of bands you like; TV shows you can't stand; or links to other Web sites you really like.

www.yourdomain.com?

Domain names are Internet addresses such as pbs.org, aol.com, and whitehouse.gov. Owning a domain name can be fairly inexpensive—often a domain name can be leased for as little as $15 per year. You may be tempted to register your own domain. Perhaps someone even registered or planned to register a domain for you as a gift. If this is the case, be aware that your personal information may be available to anyone who does something called a "whois lookup" on your domain. That is, even if you take precautions not to include any personal identifying information on your Web site, if your Web site has its own domain name, your personal information may nevertheless be exposed.

If you want your own domain name, ask your parent or another adult to register it for you. Tell the person that he or she should use a P.O. Box or a work address when registering the domain. Domain registries also require e-mail addresses. It would be a good idea to create an e-mail address hosted by a free e-mail company, such as hotmail.com, for this purpose.

Freedom of Expression

The First Amendment is the part of the United States Constitution that guarantees your right to free speech. Your right to free speech is part of a group of rights collectively called your right to freedom of expression. The First Amendment means that in order for the government to restrict your right to speak, it needs to have a pretty good reason.

The First Amendment protects your right to say what you want on your own Web site. Just because you have the right to say something, however, does not mean that you should say it. Unless you have a good reason, you should avoid publishing things that could make people angry. Also, if you use school resources in any way to build or host your Web page, the school may be able to have some control over what you can say.

Furthermore, despite what most people think, your right to free speech does not mean that you can say anything, to anyone, at any time. There are limits on what you can say, as well as how you can say it. Let's take a look at those limits so you know what to watch out for.

Fraud

Fraud includes statements of fact, opinion, or intention that someone knows—or really should have known—to be false or misleading. For instance, if you purposefully (knowingly) sold your used Nintendo game on your Web site as "new," that would be fraudulent. As you can imagine, our laws don't protect lying to people in this way as "free speech."

On the other hand, "talking up" something is not necessarily fraud. If you sell a Nintendo game as "one of the coolest games out there," even if most people wouldn't think that to be true, you probably wouldn't be committing fraud.

Defamation and Invasion of Privacy

Defamation is not protected free speech. Defamation involves publishing on your Web site (or any other form of media) something untrue about someone that injures his or her reputation, or makes other people avoid dealing with that person. The exact definition varies from state to state. Even if you are 99 percent sure that something is true, if you publish it and it turns out not to be true, you could get into serious trouble.

If you want to tell people about something that might be considered defamatory, you should just write about what you have actually observed and let people draw their own conclusions. And before you write anything at all, remember that it is important to respect people's privacy. If you don't, you could get sued for invasion of privacy.

Copyright and Trademark

Copyright is a right that Congress gives to authors, musicians, artists, computer programmers, and others who create works. It allows these people—collectively called authors—to temporarily control how their works are copied, distributed, altered, etc. This right is given to authors to encourage them to create. It is argued that if authors are not permitted to enjoy the fruits of their labors, they will not be inclined to create anything.

Trademarks are symbols, pictures, or words that businesses use to identify where their products come from and to make their products stand out. Businesses may spend large amounts of money or expend other resources to develop recognition of their trademarks. To help them protect their investments, the law allows businesses to control how their trademarks are used.

Although you have a right to free speech, taking someone's trademark or copyrighted work without his or her permission does not count as free speech. You need to be especially careful about using someone's copyrighted work on your Web page because it can be very tempting to grab an image from another site to put on your own. Even if an image does not say it is copyrighted, it may be. If you need images for your Web site, try to get ones from public domain Web sites. You should also be aware that most musicians (or their record companies) have copyrights to their recordings. That means if you download or upload an mp3, you could get sued.

Just because someone holds a copyright to a work, however, does not completely prevent you from using it. There is a legal doctrine called "fair use" that limits the rights given to authors. Under some circumstances, copies of a work may be made for criticism, comment, news reporting, teaching (including multiple copies for classroom use), scholarship, and research. Examples of fair use include publishing small excerpts of a novel in an on-line review, creating a parody of a work, and making limited copies of a work for academic study.

If you are unsure about using someone's copyrighted work, it's best to keep on the safe side. If it is possible to contact the author of the work that you would like to use, then do so. For example, if you want to use a picture from a person's Web page, you could e-mail the person to request permission to use the picture. You could also check the U.S. Copyright Office home page, at http://lcweb.loc.gov/copyright, to find out more about what is legal to use on your Web page.

For the Future

Hopefully, this book has shown you the ways in which many areas of the Internet work, alerted you to some of the dangers of the Internet, and given you guidelines about how to avoid those dangers. As you venture onto the Internet, remember that new and interesting technologies are constantly being developed and new scams are constantly being dreamed up. It is important to seek out new information about Internet safety as it becomes available.

For this reason, you should use this book as a set of guidelines rather than a set of absolute and comprehensive rules. The key to staying safe and having fun on-line is using common sense and alerting a trustworthy adult when you need help. Happy surfing!

Glossary

acronym A word formed from the initial letters of a name or phrase.

brick-and-mortar store A store that has a physical location where customers can go to shop.

cookie A bit of information sent from a Web site to a browser; the cookie is sent back to the Web site every time a page is requested from the site.

emoticons A collection of keyboard symbols that are used in unique combinations to indicate emotion.

e-tailer A store on the Internet.

filter A software program used to keep the user from accessing certain Web sites.

firewall A device or computer program designed to prevent unauthorized access to a private network or computer.

First Amendment An amendment to the United States Constitution guaranteeing the right to freedom of speech, freedom of the press, freedom of religion, and freedom of assembly, among others.

flaming Sending messages with the intent of making someone angry or upset.

incite To provoke trouble or violence.

Internet A global network made up of millions of connected computers.

ISP   An acronym for Internet service provider; a company or school that connects people or other companies to the Internet.

modem   Short for modulator-demodulator; a device that helps to transfer data between computers and to connect users to the Internet.

mp3   The filename extension for Moving Pictures Group Experts Layer 3 compressed audio files; this term has become synonymous with music files transmitted over the Internet.

netappliance   An inexpensive device created primarily to connect someone to the Internet to perform basic on-line functions, such as Web surfing or e-mailing.

netiquette   Etiquette guidelines created with the purpose of maintaining civility in cyberspace.

newbie   A user who is new to a system or service, such as a chat service.

pedophile   An adult who is sexually attracted to minors.

portal   A Web site that offers a broad array of resources and services, including the ability to search the Web for specific information.

scam   A fraudulent scheme or swindle.

search engine   A Web site that searches the Web for Web pages or other media containing special terms inputted by the user.

spam   "Junk" e-mail messages that are sent to many people at once.

World Wide Web   A network of hypertext links or hyperlinks that allows Internet users to move easily from one Web site to another.

Where to Go for Help

Organizations

In the United States
The Council of Better Business Bureau
4200 Wilson Boulevard, Suite 800
Arlington, VA 22203-1838
(703) 276-0100
Web site: http://www.bbb.org

FBI Internet Fraud Complaint Center
c/o The Federal Bureau of Investigation
J. Edgar Hoover Building
935 Pennsylvania Avenue NW
Washington, DC 20535-0001
(202) 324-3000
Web site: http://www.ifccfbi.gov

National Center for Missing and Exploited Children
Charles B. Wang International Children's Building
699 Prince Street
Alexandria, VA 22314-3175
(800) THE-LOST (843-5678)
Web site: http://www.missingkids.org

United States Department of Education
400 Maryland Avenue SW
Washington, DC 20202-0498
(800) USA-LEARN (872-5327)
Web site: http://www.ed.gov

In Canada

Canadian Centre for Occupational Health and Safety
250 Main Street East
Hamilton, ON L8N 1H6
(800) 668-4284
Web site: http://www.ccohs.ca

Web Sites

bigchalk.com: The Education Network
http://www.bigchalk.com

The Copyright Website
http://www.benedict.com

CyberAngels
http://cyberangels.org

Deja.com
http://www.deja.com

Internet Public Library Youth Division
http://www.ipl.org/youth

National Fraud Information Center
http://www.fraud.org

Netiquette Guide
http://www.albion.com/netiquette

SafeTeens.com: Teen Safety on the Internet
http://www.safeteens.com

Truth, Lies, and the Internet
http://coverage.cnet.com/Content/Features/Dlife/Truth

Webopedia: Online Computer Directory for Internet
Terms and Technical Support
http://www.webopedia.com

World Kids Network
http://www.worldkids.net

These sites provide reports on the latest viruses
http://www.ca.com
http://www.mcafee.com
http://www.symantec.com

These sites allow you to analyze e-mail headers
http://help.mindspring.com/docs/006/emailheaders
http://www.faqs.org/faqs/net-abuse-faq/spam-faq

These sites provide e-tailer ratings
http://www.bizrate.com
http://www.resellerratings.com

For Further Reading

Bruno, Bonnie. *Internet Family Fun: A Parents' Guide to Safe Surfing.* San Francisco: No Starch Press, 1997.

Burgstahler, Sheryl. *New Kids on the Net: A Tutorial for Teachers, Parents, and Students.* Boston: Allyn & Bacon, 1997.

Croft, Jennifer. *Everything You Need to Know About Staying Safe in Cyberspace.* New York: Rosen Publishing Group, 1999.

Gelman, Robert, B., and Stanton McCandlish. *Protecting Yourself Online: The Definitive Resource on Safety, Freedom, and Privacy in Cyberspace.* New York: HarperCollins, 1998.

Hafner, Katie, and Matthew Lyon. *Where Wizards Stay Up Late: The Origins of the Internet.* Carmichael, CA: Touchstone, 1998.

Levine, John R., Carol Baroudi, and Margaret Levine Young. *The Internet for Dummies* (7th ed). Foster, CA: IDG Books Worldwide, 2000.

McCormick, Anita Louise. *The Internet: Surfing the Issues.* Springfield, NJ: Enslow, 1998.

Tarbox, Katherine. *Katie.com: My Story.* New York: E.P. Dutton, 2000.

Young, Kimberly S. *Caught in the Net: How to Recognize the Signs of Internet Addiction and a Winning Strategy for Recovery.* New York: John Wiley & Sons, 1998.

Index

A

acceptable use policy (AUP), 37
America Online (AOL), 2, 15,
19, 26–27, 56, 62, 63,
64, 82, 98
antivirus programs, 19–20,
66, 67, 92
auctions
on-line, 89–91
person-to-person,
90–91

B

browsers, 7, 8, 17, 70, 77,
80, 84, 85, 86
bulletin boards, 9, 22, 30, 31,
35, 36, 100, 103

C

chat rooms, 1, 8, 15, 21, 22,
30, 31, 35, 36, 37, 68,
86, 93–100, 101, 102,
103, 104, 106
cookies, 28, 82–84, 85, 86
copyright and trademarks, 38,
110–111
credit cards, 10, 15, 16–18,
19, 88
cyberstalking, 29–30

D

data, backing it up, 21
defamation, 37, 109–110
digital subscriber line (DSL),
3, 20

domain names, 7, 17,
107–108
downloading files, 91–92
downloading music, legal
difficulties, 34, 38, 111

E

e-mail
addresses, which to
use, 101, 102, 108
attachments, 35, 3–54,
66–67, 91, 102
chain letters, 35,
63–66
conveying emotion in,
43–46, 47–48
forwarding addresses,
67–69, 102
forwarding it, 54–55,
65–66
hoaxes, 63–64
how to tell if it's fake,
57–62
jokes, 35, 65
mass mailings/spam,
50, 52–53, 60, 101
multimedia, 55–56
recipient fields, 40–42,
49, 53, 60, 61
replying to, 48–52
what it is, 6
e-mail addresses
accuracy of, 39–40
choosing, 25
emoticons, 44–46

F

filters, 78–80
firewalls, 20
First Amendment, 108–109
flaming, 30, 35–36, 103–104
forms, filling in, 27, 86–87
friends, on- and off-line,
    31–32, 98–99

H

hackers, 11, 13, 15, 17, 19

I

instant messaging, 8–9, 15,
    21–22, 26–27, 31, 34
insults, 31, 33, 34
Internet
    devices to connect to it,
    3–5
    emotions aroused on,
    30, 47–48, 103–104
    false information on,
    32, 73–75, 76, 98
    finding information on,
    71–73
    free speech and, 33,
    37, 108–109, 110
    hatred and
    discrimination on,
    75–77, 93
    infrastructure of, 2–3
    netiquette (rules of
    behavior) on, 34–37,
    50, 65, 94, 102–103

scary/dangerous
    situations on, 10,
    28–31, 57, 67, 75,
    76, 93–94, 97–100,
    101, 104–105, 111
sensitivity to others on,
    33, 34, 35, 55
service providers
    (ISPs), 2–3, 10, 15,
    16, 18, 31, 37, 56,
    58, 62, 81–82, 87,
    88, 101, 104
sexual or
    objectionable
    content on, 31, 32,
    65, 71, 75–76,
    78–79, 93, 101, 105

M

mailing lists, 8, 9, 50,
    101–103, 104
mp3 files, 9, 34, 38, 111

N

netizens, 10, 33, 104
newsgroups, 8, 9, 22, 34, 73,
    91, 100–101, 102, 104
new users/newbies, 36, 103

P

parent/adult, consulting with,
    10, 16–17, 22, 26, 28,
    29, 30, 31, 37, 48, 57,
    65, 67, 75, 76, 77, 86,
    90–91, 99–100, 101,
    104, 107

parents, educating your,
        22, 31
passwords, 10–16, 19, 56, 60
personal identification
        information, 21,
        22–24, 25, 26, 56,
        57, 65–66, 84, 86,
        87–88, 98–99, 101,
        106–107, 108
police, 29, 31, 104
privacy, 10, 21, 26, 27, 28,
        37–38, 41, 49, 62,
        65, 68, 100, 106–107
    respecting other
        people's, 36, 38, 53,
        65, 99, 110
    protecting while
        surfing Web, 21–22,
        69, 79–84
privacy policies on Web sites,
        26, 86–87
profiles, disabling, 26–27
protocols, 5–6, 92
proxy server, 80, 82
public computers, using,
        84–86

S
scams/fraud, 15, 17, 32–33,
        56, 60, 88, 91, 109
school, 1, 26, 31, 37, 79, 82,
        101, 104, 109
search engines, 31, 72, 86

shopping on-line, 16–18, 22,
        88, 89
spam, 50, 52–53, 87, 101

T
telephone, 15, 55
Trojan horse, 19

U
usernames, choosing, 24–26,
        31, 98
URL, 7, 17, 54, 63, 79, 85

V
viruses, 10, 19–20, 63,
        66–67, 92

W
Web sites
        creating them, 106–109
        finding reputable ones,
        74–75
        ones to avoid, 75–78
        opting
        out/deregistering, 28,
        84, 87–88
        secure sites, 17, 88
        what they are, 7,
        70–71
World Wide Web
        what it is, 7
        origin of, 70

www.ingramcontent.com/pod-product-compliance
Lightning Source LLC
Chambersburg PA
CBHW071221050326
40689CB00011B/2394